The Eighteenth-Century Woman

THE EIGHTEENTH-CENTURY WOMAN

Olivier Bernier

DOUBLEDAY & COMPANY, INC.
Garden City, New York
Published in association with
The Metropolitan Museum of Art, New York

To J.K.O.

who asked me to write this book,
and whose advice and encouragement
were of immeasurable help

This book was published in connection with an exhibition at The Costume Institute, The Metropolitan Museum of Art, New York, from December 16, 1981, to September 5, 1982. The exhibition was made possible by a grant from Merle Norman Cosmetics.

Jacket illustration and frontispiece: Details of a portrait of Madame de Pompadour, by Quentin de La Tour. Photograph courtesy of Musées Nationaux, Paris.

Published by
The Metropolitan Museum of Art, New York
Bradford D. Kelleher, Publisher
John P. O'Neill, Editor in Chief
Mary Barnett, Editor
Gerald Pryor, Designer

Library of Congress Cataloging in Publication Data

Bernier, Olivier.
    The eighteenth-century woman.
    "Published in connection with an exhibition at the Costume Institute, the Metropolitan Museum of Art, New York, from December 16, 1981 to September 5, 1982."
    1. Women—History—18th century. 2. Women—Biography. I. Metropolitan Museum of Art (New York, N.Y.) II. Costume Institute (New York, N.Y.) III. Title.
HQ1150.B47   1982   305.4′09′033   81-22320
ISBN 0-87099-294-5 (MMA)   AACR2
ISBN 0-385-17875-1 (Doubleday)

Acknowledgments

I am grateful to the following people for their help in researching and locating many of the illustrations that appear in this book: Ms. Olga Raggio, Chairman, Mr. James Parker, Curator, and Ms. Clare Le Corbeiller and Mr. William Rieder, Associate Curators, Department of European Sculpture and Decorative Arts, The Metropolitan Museum of Art; Mr. Lawrence Turčić, Research Associate, Department of Drawings; and Ms. Alice Zrebiec, Assistant Curator, Textile Study Room. I owe a special debt to David W. Kiehl, Assistant Curator, Department of Prints and Photographs, who was kind enough to put all the resources of his department's vast collection at my disposal.

The following photographers worked on new photography with great good will and know-how: Sheldan Collins, Lynton Gardiner, Alexander Mikhailovich, and Walter J. F. Yee, The Photograph Studio, The Metropolitan Museum of Art, and I owe special thanks to Mark D. Cooper, Manager, for his unfailing cooperation and good humor.

Ms. Amy Horbar, Editorial Assistant, Editorial Department, The Metropolitan Museum of Art, provided me with essential help throughout in obtaining photographs, accession numbers, and other vital information. Mr. Stephen Jamail, Assistant to Mrs. Vreeland, guided my steps within the Museum and thus greatly eased my task.

Mr. Ronald Freyberger was good enough to share with me his extensive knowledge of the eighteenth-century decorative arts.

The Thomas J. Watson Library, The Metropolitan Museum of Art, provided me with access to its rich research facilities. I must express my continuing sense of obligation to the New York Public Library, without whose admirable collections and helpful staff much of my research would have been impossible.

Finally, I owe a debt of gratitude to Ms. Mary Barnett, who edited this book with admirable thoroughness and patience.

Olivier Bernier

Contents

Foreword   Diana Vreeland   6

Preface   Olivier Bernier   7

Chapter 1: *The Emergence of Power*   11
            Madame des Ursins
            The duchesse de Berry

Chapter 2: *The Sway of Intelligence*   27
            Madame du Deffand
            Madame de Pompadour

Chapter 3: *Writer and Publicist*   49
            Betje Wolff
            Madame Necker

Chapter 4: *The Flesh Triumphant*   69
            Mademoiselle Clairon
            Madame du Barry

Chapter 5: *In Search of Freedom*   96
            Abigail Adams
            Georgiana, Duchess of Devonshire

Chapter 6: *Working Women*   117
            Mademoiselle Bertin
            Madame Vigée-Lebrun

Chapter 7: *To Rule a World*   143
            The margravine of Bayreuth
            Queen Maria Carolina

Source Notes   163
Selected Bibliography   167

Foreword

Courage, Gallantry, Beauty, Honor: the standards of the eighteenth century always remained in view— through war, revolution, evolution, intrigue, and dishonesty—with etiquette and order the people's companion and guide.

Everything was a form of exultation and triumph . . . trumpets, bugles, fanfares, and banners . . . splendid architecture . . . escutcheons and trophies on palace walls and on rooftops . . . graceful interiors filled with objects designed to be as useful and as beautiful as the craftsman could make them . . . spreading gardens scented with the fresh smells of nature before petrol and pollution . . . fountains like huge jets of crystal . . . barges floating down canals beneath the stars, with musicians serenading pretty women . . . the language of the streets, the language of scholars.

Everything was emerging and growing—the whisper and murmur of change were everywhere. Villages were becoming towns, towns were becoming cities, cities were dominating nations. The eighteenth-century woman in Europe and America was born into a world of opening doors, of opportunity. She came forward, walking quite naturally into the vista of promise that lay before her, translating ambition into opportunity . . . and reality.

Diana Vreeland
Special Consultant
The Costume Institute
The Metropolitan Museum of Art

Preface

"*Women reigned then,*" *Madame Vigée-Lebrun, a highly successful painter, wrote about the France of the 1770s and 1780s, and she was right. After many centuries of darkness, women came into the light during the eighteenth century. They molded public opinion, governed countries, set literary and artistic standards, made fashion a universal necessity, and ruled society. Still, they never thought they were the same as men: they required and expected to be treated with the deference, the admiration which was obviously their due.*

It wasn't that women, as in the nineteenth century, were considered fragile flowers who needed protection from the rough world outside. They hunted and rode, just like men. They chose their sexual partners freely and changed them frequently. They spent what they wished, went where they wanted, and did what amused them, whether it was giving a costume ball, attending a physics lecture, or running a salon. The maréchale de Luxembourg was a patron of writers and became Rousseau's great benefactor. Madame de Pompadour helped to start a porcelain factory. Women's lives, unhampered by obstinate husbands, were theirs to spend as they pleased.

That, at least, was the custom, although the laws that had been made centuries earlier had not changed. While it was almost unheard-of for a husband to exercise his legal powers, in theory he could do so at any time. The law assumed that a woman occupied one of four categories: she was under age (that is, under twenty-five), married, separated, or widowed. Unmarried women were a rarity, since matrimony was based on social convenience, not on mutual love. The decision to marry was made by the couple's families; after the details were settled, and only then, the bride and groom were informed. In this respect, certainly, men and women were equal: neither was consulted about marriage, and both were expected to give automatic consent to the family's choice.

Young, unmarried women were entirely in their parents' power. They were married off or, if there was no dowry, put into a convent; in either case they could only obey. Of course, a woman who was over twenty-five and had her own money could live as she chose. Since estates were usually entailed to the eldest son, however, women were not likely to be rich unless they were the last of a great family. Of course, there were some spinsters: Louis XV's daughters, Mesdames Adélaide, Louise, Sophie, and Victoire, for instance; or women like the couturiere Rose Bertin (see Chapter 6) who earned their own living. Then too, many unmarried lower-class working women—seamstresses and laundresses, for example—slept with the men they chose and produced illegitimate children.

In law, a wife owed her husband absolute obedience and fidelity but could expect very little in return. The husband chose where and how the couple was to live. He was entitled to have affairs. He could demand a perfectly run household. He alone could decide on the children's education and future careers. And if his wife was unfaithful or disobedient, he could have her confined to a convent for the rest of her life.

There was no divorce, although a wife could obtain a separation if she could prove extreme brutality, irresponsibility, or impotence. This recourse involved a long and complex procedure and was not often successful, but separation always remained a possibility. Once a separation was granted, the wife recovered her dowry and sometimes even received an income from the husband.

As for widows, they were free at last. No one could tell them what to do. On the other hand, there were few rich widows: they were likely to have their dowry plus an agreed-upon jointure paid out by the husband's heir, the eldest son. However, if there were no children and the husband's estate did not pass to another male relative, the widow did inherit it.

Perhaps the most remarkable feature of this legal framework was its growing irrelevance. In all, probably fewer than a dozen women were actually sent off to a convent because they were adulterous. Husbands, who were constantly unfaithful, expected their wives to live just as freely. Most marriages could be characterized as a distant partnership of equals. In fact, though not in law, women were as free as they are today—with one great exception: divorce.

But what about money? Legally women could own, inherit, and bequeath estates—everything, in fact, except titles of nobility. Rich spinsters and widows could dispose of their property freely, but married women were in their husbands' power. Marriage in the absence of a dowry was almost inconceivable. (In aristocratic families without quite enough money, any extra daughter simply became a nun.) Dowries were required even in lower-class marriages, although the property might consist only of a few dresses and some bed linens. On the other hand, rank was sometimes a substitute for money among the nobility; when La Fayette married Adrienne de Noailles, for example, her dowry was small because she was the daughter of a powerful duke.

The marriage contract usually stipulated that the wife could dispose of the income from her dowry and that if she was widowed or separated, the capital returned to her and then passed to her children. As long as she was married, however, she had no control over the capital and very little recourse if her husband chose to dissipate it. In the upper classes, where everyone contracted debts, women in fact bought whatever they wanted and never gave payment a thought. In the middle and lower classes, wives often managed the family budget while their husbands earned a living.

A new relationship between women and money emerged during the eighteenth century: for the first time, many women began to earn their own. They became clothing designers like Rose Bertin (Chapter 6), painters like Mme Vigée-Lebrun (Chapter 6), writers like Betje Wolff (Chapter 3), and actresses like Mademoiselle Clairon (Chapter 4).* Quite often they owned small shops or managed the books and the cash register in their husband's business. Thus it became possible for a woman to make her own way without being a prostitute or a laundress.

As for children, in the upper classes, at least, they hardly existed. Every wife understood that she must produce a male heir, but once the baby was born, it was usually sent off to some village nurse and quite forgotten. When the child was six or seven, it was brought back to its family, given a tutor or gover-

---

*Throughout the book, the author has followed the local usage of the period in regard to names and titles.

ness, and again forgotten. Around the age of ten or eleven, girls went off to a convent to receive an education of sorts and wait for a husband, while boys were taught to ride, fence, and dance. All this changed after the publication of Rousseau's Emile. In the late seventies and eighties, it suddenly became fashionable to care about children. Noble mothers were seen to breastfeed their babies, competent tutors were hired, and children were actually considered human. Even so, most upper-class parents regarded childbearing and child rearing as disagreeable necessities.

None of this was true in the middle classes, where children represented the family's chance for improvement. Bourgeois children were kept at home when young, sent to excellent schools later, and always given love and attention.

It would be misleading to judge women's status during this period too strictly according to legal rights. In fact, the eighteenth-century woman was both powerful and free. Better still, she was constantly courted—some said worshiped—and she expected to live a life of pleasure in the most beautiful of settings. Never, perhaps, have people enjoyed more elegant decor or worn more splendid clothes. In rooms decorated with admirably sculpted paneling and furniture carved by cabinetmakers of genius, the eighteenth-century woman ruled over her admirers. Of course, there were inconveniences: it cannot have been comfortable to wear boned corsets and hooped skirts or, in the seventies, towering hairdos so complex that they could not be taken down at night. Moreover, Versailles, like every other court, required long hours of waiting and standing. Still, luxury reached unparalleled heights and even middle-class women lived better, and in pleasanter surroundings, than ever before.

How did a well-to-do woman spend her day? Unless there was a court function she had to attend, she rose late. After drinking a cup of chocolate in bed, she went through her first, private toilette. Then the doors opened to her little court of admirers. Sitting at her dressing table in corset and short petticoat, our lady chatted with them while the long process of the toilette was completed. At this time tradespeople came to offer their wares, new coiffures were invented, and the day's gossip was exchanged.

After a ride, perhaps in the Bois de Boulogne, came dinner, eaten between four and six, and then the theater, the Opéra, or a ball. The day ended with a late supper at eleven or midnight. A lecture, a drive, or a visit to the fashionable shops might be squeezed into the early afternoon. And of course, court must be paid to royalty.

It was nice to be young and pretty, since beauty was in itself a source of fame, and young women were avidly courted. Age brought its own privileges, however. Admiration was replaced by respect and extreme courtesy; the older woman's influence did not necessarily decline. No salon would have been complete without its group of elderly ladies who, among universal deference, made sharp appraisals of new customs and younger people.

This sudden blossoming, this startling rise in the power of women, appeared in an age when intelligence, culture, and manners had at last become more important than brute force. Since refinement and luxury were now necessities, since wit and manners were indispensable to the good life, obviously women were bound to rule. Sometimes it was only over a salon; but in France the salons molded opinion, helped ministers to power, even determined the government's policy. And to the east, Maria Theresa of Austria, like Catherine the Great of Russia, gave abundant proof that women were competent to rule great empires.

Mme des Ursins (Chapter 1) was not of royal birth, yet she used her court position to govern Spain and its empire for some fourteen years; she even went so far as to resist Louis XIV's direct commands. Fifty years earlier all this would have been impossible, but in 1700, as the Enlightenment took shape, the world began to change. Men had prevailed long enough. Now it was time for the eighteenth-century woman to take her place in the center of the world's stage.

O.B.

1

The Emergence of Power

Madame des Ursins
The duchesse de Berry

The physical configuration of Europe in 1700 seemed firmly established; but then, all in one day, the Pyrenees were gone. Charles II—King of Spain and the Indies, successor to Charles V* and Philip II, and the last of the Spanish Hapsburgs—had died and left his vast empire to France.

The war that followed divided the Western world: against France and Spain all the other great powers coalesced. Soon French armies were in retreat everywhere; an Austrian archduke was at Madrid; enemy raiders came within twenty miles of Versailles. Yet in a little town of northern Spain, the will to resist never faltered and streams of letters poured out to encourage the fainthearted.

> Is it indeed possible, Madame, that all the men you know feel they have their backs against the wall? Can none of them imagine new solutions? That would be a mark of their abasement such as would do them no honor; for, no matter how badly the affairs of State may go, great minds and great courages steel themselves against their ill fortune. God may perform miracles when he pleases; I am praying that he may reawaken those feelings of hope which have so completely disappeared from your court.

These proud words were sent in 1709 by a woman to a woman, and both were in positions of great power. The writer was the princesse des Ursins, prime minister of Spain in all but title; her exhortation was addressed to Madame de Maintenon, the secret wife of Louis XIV of France. Time-honored opinion might have been that men are meant to rule; but as the new century began, the fate of Europe often rested on the shoulders of these two women.

When, in 1700, the Spanish empire was willed to France, it was only after a good deal of soul-searching that Louis XIV decided to accept the legacy on behalf of his grandson, the duc d'Anjou,

*The emperor Charles V was actually Charles I of Spain.

Houasse (attributed to). *Mme des Ursins.*
Musée Lambinet, Versailles

although he knew that war would follow, and that Spain would have to be governed by a French ambassador. For the new Spanish King, who called himself Philip V, was no ruler but a slow, pious teen-ager obsessed with hunting and sex.

Still, a wife must be found for Philip, and Louis XIV chose Maria Luisa of Savoy. The next step was to select a *camarera mayor,* the senior court official who ran the Queen's Household, decided disputed points of etiquette, and virtually never left her mistress. What better way to know what was going on at the Spanish court, Louis thought, than to appoint a Frenchwoman to this post?

The office of *camarera mayor,* always important, was now crucial because Philip's new wife was quite likely to be anti-French. Maria Luisa's father, the duke of Savoy, ruled over the Alpine passes and played a major role in European politics; hence the marriage. But proximity notwithstanding, he was no friend of France. Louis XIV hoped, of course, that once Maria Luisa sat on the Spanish throne, the duke would defend her interests. On the other hand, he might come up with some complex, nefarious scheme through which Austria would rule Spain and the new monarchs some portion of Italy conveniently close to Savoy. The princess was only twelve years old: some strong-minded, yet pleasant, woman must be found to mold her adolescent ideas. After much searching, it was Mme de Maintenon who came up with an old acquaintance—a woman she had known some thirty years earlier, whose first husband was long dead, and whose second husband, Prince Orsini (gallicized to des Ursins) had also conveniently passed on. Mme des Ursins was French but had lived in Spain and Italy; she was intelligent, wellborn but relatively poor; she hungered for a great court position. Mme de Maintenon, who understood power, knew that through Mme des Ursins, she herself would become a conduit for the Sun King's Spanish policy. So she lobbied Louis XIV, convinced him, and wrote the French ambassador in Madrid: "[Mme des Ursins] is witty, kind, polite, and understands foreigners; she has always held great positions, has been loved everywhere, and is a Grandee of Spain;

but she is also without husband or children, and so will not ask for much. . . . I think her more appropriate for what you want than any woman I know here."

Mme de Maintenon was quite right as far as that went, but there was a great deal more to Mme des Ursins. In a time when an upper-class woman's life tended to follow rather conventional lines—an early marriage, a position at court, years of intrigue and overspending, with always the hope of seducing the King—Mme des Ursins's had been like the kind of improbable novel which Mlle de Scudéry had made popular a few years before.

Anne Marie de La Trémoille was born in 1642 to one of the greatest French aristocratic families. At the age of seventeen she was married to the comte de Chalais, scion of another great family. The future seemed predictable: he was handsome, she was pretty, and they lived the life of any well-to-do young couple at court. There were balls and late suppers, masquerades and hunts, attendance on the twenty-one-year-old Louis XIV, but they also enjoyed the fashionable intellectual gatherings in Paris, where a brilliant but impoverished young woman, Mme Scarron, shone in spite of her marriage to an improvident and impotent poet.

Then suddenly Chalais had to flee the country, all because of a silly little law. Duels, as any well-bred young man could tell you, were the stuff of life; they were fun, they required skill, they gave you a delicious sense of danger; only, they were now quite forbidden. Safe in the knowledge that such a pedestrian restraint applied only to others, M. de Chalais dueled with an acquaintance, M. de La Frette, and ran him through. Duels had been illegal for some forty years, but the law was no longer obeyed by the aristocracy because of the general laxity which had followed the recently ended civil war. Now, to everyone's surprise, Louis XIV announced that the law would be enforced: M. de Chalais had just committed murder. Chalais, who assumed that the King's anger would soon fade, went to Spain and confidently awaited his pardon. To everyone's surprise, his wife joined him.

Louis XIV, however, saw this as a test case; and he had a horror of being disobeyed, so he made it plain that he never wanted to hear about the Chalais again—especially the silly young wife who had left his court to join her husband, of all people. Time passed. Mme de Chalais learned to speak Spanish and to complain about the dullness of the Madrileños. Then it became obvious that France and Spain would soon be at war. Once more the Chalais fled, this time to Italy. They had just reached Mestre, on the lagoon opposite Venice, when the young comte caught a pernicious fever. A few days later, he was dead.

Suddenly Mme de Chalais was both alone and penniless. She still wasn't wanted back in France, so there was nothing for it but to retreat to a Roman convent, with no apparent hope of remarriage. It was years before she came out, at the instigation of the French ambassador, to marry Don Flavio Orsini, duke of Bracciano and the greatest of the Roman nobles.

Of course, there were drawbacks. Don Flavio was old, gouty, and, although he owned huge estates, pressed for cash. Mme de Chalais's parents had died and left her money, and the duke wrangled over her dowry for almost a year before the marriage took place. But its first, its best consequence was that the new Princess Orsini found herself back in Louis XIV's good graces. Rome was rent between pro-French and pro-Spanish factions, and by marrying a Frenchwoman who had made it plain that she would obey her King's every wish, Don Flavio provided the city with a French first lady.

Once again the new princess's life seemed predictable. She would save what she could of the Orsini fortune, rule over the grandest palace in Rome, and give parties for Louis XIV's birthday. Then Don Flavio died. Suddenly the creditors closed in; the palace was almost sold and, once again, the princess was penniless and frantic. She remained afloat only through intrigue, long, long letters to Versailles, conferences with the French ambassador, and cleverly managed audiences with the Pope. It was a sad position for a woman of fifty-six: it seemed that only senility and death remained. This was not her view, however; Princess Orsini might plot, scheme, and complain, but it was obvious to everyone that she was enjoying every moment of her life.

In another age Mme des Ursins would have been a best-selling writer. Her letters are racy, descriptive, vivid, frequently funny. Here is her account of a scene that took place in 1701:

> I have the honor to take the King of Spain's robe when he goes to bed, and to give it back to him with his slippers when he rises in the morning. So far, I can be patient; but every night, when the King goes into the Queen's room, the count of Benevente loads me down with His Majesty's sword, a chamberpot and [an oil] lamp the contents of which I usually spill all over my dress: it is really too grotesque. . . . Recently, the lamp went out because I had spilled out half its oil; since we had arrived at night, I had never seen the windows and did not know where they were; I nearly broke my nose bumping into the wall, and it took us, the King of Spain and I, almost fifteen minutes of stumbling in the dark before we found one of the windows.

Then, too, Mme des Ursins sees through pretense and pompousness while acknowledging real talent. Her letters are also full of convincing arguments: the French ambassador (with whom she had quarreled) must be recalled, certain cardinals must be courted, stratagems must be used. By the time we turn the last page of the first volume of her letters, we understand more about the late seventeenth century than ten history books could tell us.

Of course, the princess had a problem: she was forbidden by etiquette to write the King directly. Luckily, her old acquaintance from Parisian intellectual circles, Mme Scarron, who had been created marquise de Maintenon after many years of widowhood, was now secretly married to the monarch himself. Besides, Mme de Maintenon's niece was married to the duc de Noailles, who was one of the princess's oldest friends. It all worked very nicely and, ecstatic though she was, Mme des Ursins was perhaps not very surprised when, on April 20, 1701, Torcy, the French foreign minister, announced her appointment as *camarera mayor*.

"I hardly know how to convey the excess of my joy," she wrote him. "Either our language lacks sufficiently strong expressions, or my mind is so dazed by the news that I cannot even begin to explain my feelings at present." At fifty-nine Mme des Ursins was, at long last, beginning to live.

"She had vast ambitions which went far beyond . . . those common to her sex," wrote Saint-Simon, the great memorialist, and he knew her well. The new *camarera mayor* would have to reorganize the court, reform the old, stultifying Spanish etiquette, and manage the Queen's Household. For Mme des Ursins, however, this was only a preface to the tasks of winning the war and running the country.

She set off to meet the new Queen with a proper cortege. Surrounding her were eight gentlemen-in-waiting, six pages, an almoner, twelve footmen, and a cloud of other servants, all dressed in new gold-braided livery and following two gilded, sculpted carriages. Still, she wrote, she would do better once she was settled in Spain. And perhaps all the splendor proved a comfort when she actually met Maria Luisa, for what she found was a precocious, sulky twelve-year-old, surrounded by a Savoyard court and fully prepared to resist the dangerous Frenchwoman who was being thrust upon her.

Just how well Maria Luisa had been indoctrinated became plain during her wedding night. Firmly resisting the King's advances, she insisted on talking her father's brand of politics right through the night. Philip was furious and frustrated, so the next night, firmly ignoring his bride, he turned his back on her and went to sleep. It took all Mme des Ursins's tact and cleverness to convince the youngsters that they had better things to do in bed than sulk. The following night, when the marriage was consummated, the *camarera mayor*'s power was firmly established.

Soon Louis XIV and Mme de Maintenon discovered what they had achieved. Not only did the princess do all that was expected of her while sparing Spanish susceptibilities, but, at every turn, she convinced the Queen that Versailles was right. The Queen, in turn, convinced the King.

Soon Philip went off to Italy, where the Spanish possessions were under attack. Though Maria Luisa was appointed Regent, it was Mme des Ursins who was ruling Spain and its armies.

Of course, the princess was devoted to the new dynasty and to France, but as one historian has remarked, when "the princess dealt with the weak Philip V, then her anxiety to serve gave way to a taste for domination." In fact, the King hardly realized what was going on. Only he and Mme des Ursins had access to the Queen's bedroom; once he was there, he naturally discussed the war; the Queen, who had been prompted by Mme des Ursins, made suggestions; the princess defended them; and the King, acquiescing, went out and informed his council. If by any chance the King disagreed, Maria Luisa refused to have sex. This was more than Philip could stand, since repeated daily intercourse was the only thing that kept depression at bay. After a few hours the Queen would carry her point.

This was all very well for Madrid; but far away in Versailles (messengers sometimes took as much as three weeks to make the journey) the Sun King ruled, and he expected perfect obedience. At first he got it. Torcy, the foreign minister, and Mme de Maintenon would write the princess and tell her what line to follow. By return mail, they would receive her assurances that their instructions had been carried out. Soon, however, Mme des Ursins began to feel that being on the spot, she sometimes understood the situation better than the French; surely it was best for all concerned if she simply took over.

She was right, of course, but the French ambassador, the cardinal d'Estrées, felt bypassed and powerless and so complained to Versailles that the princess was trying to run Spain single-handedly. For his part, the Sun King's original assessment of Mme des Ursins as a disobedient, rebellious young woman had been suspended but not forgotten. Thus when the affairs of the *tonsillo* and the *golilla* exploded, it became obvious to both Louis XIV and Torcy that the princess was up to her old tricks.

Court dress in Spain had changed very little since the beginning of the previous century. To the fashion-conscious French, the Spanish attire was simply grotesque—another symptom of the blindness to the modern world which had caused that country's decadence. In short order, therefore, Queen Maria Luisa decreed that ladies at court were to stop wearing the long, apronlike overskirt with which they covered their dresses. Those *tonsillos* had been originally devised to cover the feet of the Spanish ladies when, as was the custom, they sat on the ground. With the Bourbons came chairs; *tonsillos* were thus not only dowdy but useless. Yet when they were banned, the outcry was immense. Grandees muttered darkly that their wives might as well be nude: who could tell what a man might do if he caught sight of a shapely toe? Letters came promptly from Versailles telling the Queen to rescind the ban: she was needlessly antagonizing her new subjects.

Then the King gave up wearing the *golilla*— the stiff, starched, dish-shaped collar that men wear in the paintings of Velasquez—and replaced it with a lace cravat. It was all too much. The already affronted grandees, clutching desperately at their necks, protested frantically, but to no avail. The monarchs, with teen-age rashness, stood firm; the *tonsillo* and the *golilla* would have to go.

It may all seem rather like a joke to us; but in a century when etiquette was the visible representation of power, court costume could indeed arouse passion. Louis XIV, who wanted his grandson to be popular, took the complaints very seriously. Torcy soon wrote Mme des Ursins ordering the reinstatement of both articles of clothing.

Here was an obvious example, the princess felt, of a mistake due to distance. She disregarded Versailles's instructions; Louis XIV's displeasure increased. The cardinal d'Estrées sent a flood of dispatches saying that Mme des Ursins was deliberately isolating the royal couple so that she could run the country unhampered. Why, even he, a cardinal and an ambassador, was denied access to the Queen's bedroom. Of course, Mme des Ursins was writing Versailles also, claiming that it was d'Estrées who was trying to seize the government, and that in so doing he was gravely offending the

Spaniards. But it was an unequal fight. The cardinal, after all, was the King's direct representative; by opposing him Mme des Ursins was in effect defying his master. Louis XIV's horror of being disobeyed had not abated, as Torcy made very plain: "Where now are the good behavior, the excellent spirit with which we were so pleased?" he wrote her. "His Majesty could not abandon M. le cardinal d'Estrées even if he were not as pleased with his services as he actually is. . . . Imagine, therefore, the arms you are giving your enemies."

This was all bad enough; but when the princess stole and read a letter from d'Estrées to the King, she sealed her doom. Louis XIV instantly wrote Philip V and ordered him to fire Mme des Ursins. The grandson obeyed, and early in '704 the *camarera mayor* was sent back to the border.

It was obvious to everyone that the dismissal was final. Louis XIV was notoriously inflexible; the princess was sixty-two years old; she would just have to spend her declining years away from the court in boredom and isolation. When, therefore, Mme des Ursins appeared at Versailles within nine months, the court rang with speculation. It was all the more astonishing when, after a long chat with Mme de Maintenon, the princess was joined by the King himself and given the enormous honor of a lengthy private interview. The next morning Torcy wrote to the French commander in Spain: "I may tell you that the King found her as intelligent as she really is and that His Majesty is satisfied with her conversation and with the explanations she provided." It seemed incredible. Even the shrewdest observers failed to understand the King's reversal; yet its causes were simplicity itself.

First, of course, there had been the clamor of the Queen of Spain, begging for Mme des Ursins's return and obstinately refusing to appoint another *camarera mayor*. Second, a French army was badly beaten at Höchstädt. Clearly Philip and Maria Luisa were essential if Spain was to be defended; yet here they were, furious with France for sending away their beloved princess. Worse, they were floundering hopelessly without anyone to guide them. When Mme des Ursins declared in letter

Rigaud. *View of Marly,* the scene of Mme des Ursins's great triumph. The Royal Pavilion is at the top.

The Metropolitan Museum of Art, New York. Harris Brisbane Dick Fund, 1953 (53.600.1230)

after letter that her only goal in life was to please Louis XIV, that her apparent disobedience was caused solely by her efforts to further the French cause, then even the Sun King had good reason to forgive the errant lady.

Never, perhaps, did the princess enjoy her-self so much as during her five-month-long visit to Versailles. Not only was she back in the center of the civilized world, but she was also in high favor. Daily the King closeted himself with her to discuss Spain and the war. At Marly she was placed with the royal family itself—an unheard-

avec Privilege du Roy

of honor—and allowed to break a firm rule by inviting the Spanish ambassador, one of her ardent supporters, to attend the festivities. Her brother, the marquis de Noirmoutiers, was created a duke. Her nephew, the abbé de La Trémoille, was promised a cardinal's hat. Even better, a new French ambassador to Madrid was appointed at her request. The memoranda she submitted on policy, personnel, and the management of the court in Spain were all approved by the King. She asked for, and obtained, a written agreement defining her position and her powers. Best of all, Mme de

Maintenon swore eternal friendship and promised to serve as the link between Louis XIV and Mme des Ursins, so that the princess would always have the King's ear.

As for Philip and Maria Luisa, they were ecstatic. The maréchal de Tessé witnessed the long-awaited reunion on August 5, 1705, and wrote Louis XIV: "The meeting was marked by dignity, joy, and friendliness on one side, and a sort of respect and emotion on the other such that their sum is indescribable." So with everyone's agreement, Mme des Ursins became the unofficial prime minister of Spain. The solidity of her new position was made manifest when a quarrel arose over etiquette; this time Torcy promptly backed Mme des Ursins.

Clearly, nothing could go wrong anymore. And nothing did, except the war. From 1706 to 1709 the French and Spanish armies suffered defeat after defeat. Madrid was conquered by the Austrian pretender; money, troops, even bread were so scarce that there were days when the Queen herself went hungry. Then the situation improved within Spain itself when Segovia, Cadiz, and Andalusia declared for Philip V. In April, 1707, the Franco-Spanish troops won a key victory at Almanza, and in August the Queen gave birth to a son.

But everywhere else, the allies—Austria, England, and Holland—were triumphant. France's armies were beaten, her coffers empty, her provinces fast becoming deserts. As early as 1706 Mme de Maintenon wrote the princess: "Our two Kings uphold religion and justice, but they fail; our enemies attack both and they triumph. . . . The King is courageous. . . . As for me, Madame, I am but a woman and among the weakest." In August, 1707, she wrote, "It is no life to be always in such alarms." By September, 1709, she was making herself plainer still: "I have received, Madame, with kind feelings the letter full of fire and blood you were good enough to write me on the first of this month. . . . We have reason to think we have brought you [Spain] misfortune and that you will do better on your own." The meaning was obvious: Mme de Maintenon was ready to conclude a separate peace for France and

allow Spain to sink undefended. The friend had turned into a foe.

Like every other well-informed person, Mme des Ursins knew that Mme de Maintenon was always ready to abandon her friends and the policies they stood for the moment they became a liability. Suddenly this powerful secret wife was representing herself as a helpless, sick old lady who had given up politics. All untrue, of course; she simply wanted to preserve her influence on Louis XIV by rejecting whatever party at court seemed to be failing. Quite aware that she had been discarded along with Spain, Mme des Ursins fought back. Her letters to Versailles, fiery as ever, became tinged with contempt.

"We hear such dreadful things [about the conditions for peace]," she wrote in June, 1709, "that it is impossible anyone should be willing to pay such a price, or that the King's subjects would hesitate to sacrifice all they can to spare France such terrible shame." And again in October: "You will be really surprised, Madame, when despite all the measures aimed at losing Spain, you find that it keeps itself for Philip V."

Mme de Maintenon was hardly alone, though, in her despair. All through those dreadful years, only two people went on believing and fighting without fail: the seventy-one-year-old Louis XIV and the sixty-seven-year-old princesse des Ursins. In Spain it was the princess who raised money and found supplies for the armies, who encouraged the King when he was low, sent him off to lead his troops, ran the government, appointed and changed ministers. She ruled the court and reported back to Versailles, praising, criticizing, exhorting. She carried out major reforms that centralized the government and made Spain easier to rule. She looked after the brave young Queen, who was becoming sicker year by year with every child she bore. She supervised the care and education of the royal children. And still Mme des Ursins had time to improve the old Alcazar Palace in Madrid so that the King and Queen could be a little more comfortable, all the while consulting French doctors about Maria Luisa's mysteriously swelling glands. When the Treaty of Utrecht was finally drafted, everyone knew that Philip V would not have kept his throne without Mme des Ursins.

Nor did the King show himself ungrateful: he asked the princess what she wanted. A small sovereign principality, she answered, nothing grand or extravagant, just a few square miles with a reasonable income, a place where she could be wholly self-sufficient and fear no one's whim. Accordingly Philip V refused to sign the treaty unless it included Mme des Ursins's principality. By the time it became obvious, two years later, that the princess would not have her wish, France and Spain were practically at war over this issue. The *camarera mayor* was quite out of favor with Louis XIV. Still, it hardly seemed to matter: Their Catholic Majesties were devoted to her, she was surrounded with nieces and nephews who had been given lush appointments; the ministers were in her pocket. Versailles could just go on grumbling.

Nothing, it seemed, could threaten her position. When Queen Maria Luisa died of tuberculosis in February, 1714, the office of *camarera mayor* automatically became extinct. So the King named Mme des Ursins governess of the royal children and, in his grief, refused to see anyone except her. In no time, it was rumored that she wanted to become Queen of Spain. In fact she was frantically searching for an appropriate young princess, since it was clear that the King could not long remain celibate without going mad. He was too pious to take a mistress; a wife was vitally necessary.

The new Queen must be meek enough to obey Mme des Ursins; a Hapsburg, for instance, would obviously not do. As it turned out, the envoy from Parma, the abbé Alberoni, had a princess to suggest. She was not very pretty, or very young, or very clever. She would, he said, be not only perfectly suitable but eternally grateful. So without wasting a moment, Mme des Ursins arranged the match and sent for Elisabeth of Parma. As soon as the bride approached Spain, Mme des Ursins, *camarera mayor* once again, went to receive her. The meeting took place on a freezing December night at Alcalá de Henares in northern Spain. There, the princess was seen to curtsy to the new Queen as she stepped out of her carriage. The two

women went upstairs and were closeted together. Soon raised voices were heard, and the door opened. "Arrest that woman!" shouted Elisabeth, pointing to Mme des Ursins. Within an hour, still in court dress and without even a cloak, the princess was thrown into a carriage and sent over the French border. She never saw Spain again.

Amazement at such a reversal of fortune was unbounded. No one could understand what had happened. Saint-Simon, who was usually well informed, thought it was due to Mme de Maintenon's jealousy. The truth was much simpler: the new Queen was enormously ambitious, and so was her sponsor, the abbé Alberoni. He wanted to be prime minister, she wanted to rule the King, and neither could succeed if Mme des Ursins was around. So the new Queen pretended she had been insulted, and the King was far too anxious for the conjugal bed to argue. In less than ten minutes the woman who had defied Europe and ruled an empire had become another purposeless exile, not very rich and quite powerless. Another woman had vanquished her. Still, she had won universal fame, thoroughly enjoyed her years of rule, and proved that a woman could govern a country even if she had not been born on the steps of a throne.

The duchesse de Berry

Marie Louise Elisabeth d'Orléans, duchesse de Berry, achieved fame almost equal to Mme des Ursins's even though the duchess died at twenty-four. Mme des Ursins understood power; the duchesse de Berry won the right to behave just like most of the men around her.

Mademoiselle d'Orléans, the daughter of Louis XIV's nephew, the duc d'Orléans, at first seemed destined for the conventional life of a princess of the blood royal. An exceptionally intelligent little girl, she became her father's favorite when, ignoring the murderously incompetent court doctors, he single-handedly pulled her through a bout of smallpox. By the age of ten she was overweight, willful, and extremely proud of belonging to the royal family. She also kept her eyes wide open and quickly perceived the importance of rank and the necessity of winning the King's favor.

The court which buzzed around the aging Sun King in the great palace of Versailles clearly understood that it was the center of the universe. There was no life worth living elsewhere, and as soon as she was presented to her grand-uncle Louis in 1707, the twelve-year-old Mlle d'Orléans knew without a doubt that she wanted to shine in that ferocious assemblage of proud and predatory aristocrats.

At first this ambition seemed impossible. In order to achieve it, she would need to marry the duc de Berry, the King's youngest grandson, an amiable if illiterate young man. One of his two older brothers, the duc de Bourgogne, was second in line to the throne. The other had become Philip V of Spain.* Queen Marie Thérèse and her daughter-in-law, the Dauphine, had long been dead; the duchesse de Berry would therefore become the second lady in France.

---

*Louis XIV had only one son, the Grand Dauphin, who fathered these three sons. "Dauphin" was the official title of the heir to the throne.

Normally a foreign princess would have been chosen for the duke, but in 1710 that was out of the question because of the European war. As the King looked at the list of available French princesses, everyone thought that he would reject Mlle d'Orléans out of hand. First, Louis XIV didn't much like her father. The duc d'Orléans was a careless courtier who preferred his palace in Paris to the empty rounds of life at Versailles. He was constantly, grossly, notoriously unfaithful to his wife, who happened to be one of the King's cherished illegitimate children. While fighting in Spain a few years earlier, the duke had made an obscene (and promptly reported) toast to Mme de Maintenon. Moreover, he had earned the lasting enmity of the Dauphin by listening to a proposition from a group who wanted him to replace Philip V on the Spanish throne. The Dauphin could hardly be asked for his consent to a wedding between his youngest son and the duc d'Orléans's daughter.

Still, the Orléans faction had some hidden strengths. The duchess was, after all, the King's daughter. Then there was the King's mania for keeping all power to himself. The other candidate's mother, the duchesse de Bourbon, was boasting that her daughter would win because she herself was so close to the Dauphin. As soon as Louis XIV began to suspect that his relatives were trying to decide something for themselves, he acted. Calling in his son, he "talked to him like a father and like a King." After that there was nothing left but to announce the engagement.

Of course, Mlle d'Orléans had followed the complexities of the plotting. She even went on a strict diet when she heard that the King considered her too fat, no mean sacrifice for a fourteen-year-old girl who loved food; and her joy at the engagement was unbounded. "Her wit, her grace, her eloquence, the dignity and appropriateness of her terms [as she thanked me]," wrote Saint-Simon, one of the main architects of the match, "surprised me greatly, mixed as they were with bursts . . . of joy which she didn't try to conceal from me." On July 7, 1710, Mlle d'Orléans, dazzling in a gown of silver moiré covered with diamonds, became the duchesse de Berry.

Now she was seeing her dreams come true. Her sister-in-law, the duchesse de Bourgogne, alone took precedence over her: even her mother, even her grandmother, who was the King's sister-in-law, had to walk behind her. One day her husband would be the new King's only brother at the French court; in the meantime, there was nothing but pleasure ahead.

Then to everyone's shock, the new duchess started to complain. Money was short because of the war, and she was outraged that she and her husband were not given their own splendid establishment but had to share the Bourgognes' Household. Further, Louis XIV's wedding present to her was a mere 73,000 livres' worth of jewelry (approximately equivalent to $500,000), although it was true that her husband had been given 300,000 livres' worth ($1,800,000) which she could also wear. Finally, she announced, her husband was a bore.

Although the King himself was apt to behave unconventionally—after all, he was surrounded by a brood of officially recognized bastards—and although his brother, Monsieur (the duchess's grandfather), a little man with high heels and a rouged face, had a well-known taste for pretty boys, royal princesses were expected to be models of propriety. So when, shortly after her wedding, the duchess was seen to get dead drunk at a supper with her father, everyone professed great shock. In fact, the young woman was surrounded by people who thought pleasure was the only law. She had watched her father's parade of mistresses, heard all about the multiple affairs, greed, and excesses of almost everyone at court. It never occurred to her that she wasn't entitled to behave in precisely the same way.

Until the eighteenth century, the inferiority of women had been so firmly established that the accompanying double standard remained unquestioned. Now a fifteen-year-old girl was taking it for granted that she was as good as any man. She was ambitious (a quality admired in men but despised in women), so it made sense for her to join her father-in-law's little set. After all, Louis XIV was seventy-two; the Dauphin would soon be King. The problem was that her strategy looked

Gold and diamond Spanish pin.
The Metropolitan Museum of Art, New York.
Gift of Marguerite McBey, 1980 (1980.343.8)

like treason. The Dauphin's coterie, which had sponsored Mlle de Bourbon, loathed the little group around the duc de Bourgogne and the Orléans. If a man had followed her policy in that ferocious court, it would have been considered a perfectly natural attempt to rise, but in a woman it was seen as shocking and wrong.

As it turned out, the duchess's maneuver did not succeed, for the Dauphin died in 1711. "Madame la duchesse de Berry was beside herself," Saint-Simon wrote. "The bitterest despair was mixed with horror in her expression. One could see on her face a rage of sorrow, caused not by friendship but by self-interest; tearless moments, but deep and grim, were followed by a flood of tears and involuntary gestures which were signs of the extreme bitterness caused by a deep meditation." Saint-Simon is really telling us that she got what she deserved. "Suddenly she saw all her plans going up in smoke and found herself dependent on a princess [the duchesse de Bourgogne] to whom she had manifested the blackest, the most constant, the least motivated ingratitude, a princess who delighted both the King and

Rigaud. *The Gardens of the Luxembourg.* Soon after moving to the palace (in the background),
the duchesse de Berry gravely offended the Parisians when she closed the gardens to the public.
The Metropolitan Museum of Art, New York. Harris Brisbane Dick Fund, 1953 (53.600.1182)

Mme de Maintenon and who now, without hindrance, would begin to reign without waiting for the throne. . . . All those plots to which she [the duchesse de Berry] had sacrificed her soul . . . had become completely useless."

It is true that perfect fidelity to the Bourgognes might have prevented Mme de Berry from ingratiating herself with her now defunct father-in-law; but what was an ambitious and intelligent person to do? The duchesse de Berry has always had a bad press. Certainly she was self-involved; she plotted; she drank too much. According to

Saint-Simon:

She was a prodigy of wit, of pride, of ingratitude, and of folly; she was one also of debauchery and obstinacy. She had barely been married a week when she started to reveal these qualities, although her supreme falseness—and she was proud of it, considering it a great talent—sometimes concealed them, when her mood allowed it. Her rancor at having a bastard for a mother soon became obvious, along with her resentment at having had to be polite to her . . . as did her contempt for M. le duc d'Orléans's weakness and her confidence in her ability to rule him.

With manifest enjoyment, all her contemporaries dwell on her pride, her drunkenness, her debauchery. She could not altogether let herself go, however; Louis XIV might be old, but he still terrified his family. She had to pretend to like her husband, although she was soon unfaithful to him.

Then within a year the duc and duchesse de Bourgogne both died, leaving a frail two-year-old child as the sole heir to the throne. Suddenly Mme de Berry outranked everyone. She was given the Queen's apartment at Versailles, more money, more jewelry. And within another two years an obviously friendly fate disposed of the duc de Berry, who died as the result of a hunting accident. Now she was free, except for the tired old King; and as a bonus she inherited all the duke's jewels; now her collection was unrivaled. Best of all, her father, the duc d'Orléans, was the only male left alive in the immediate royal family. Clearly he would be Regent when Louis XIV died, and the duchesse de Berry's power would be absolute.

She had only a year to wait, for the King died in September, 1715. Now no one could stop her—especially not her father, whose fondness for her seemed compounded in equal parts of realism and weakness.

The spirit of the times seemed in tune with France's new first lady. After the long, repressive reign of the Sun King, the Regency was marked by an explosion of pleasure, in tone not unlike that of the 1920s. Having fun was everything; morals, conventions, rules were overthrown as the Regent set the mood. Every night he closed the doors on the business of state and presided over orgiastic suppers attended by bold young men and pretty, easy women. The evenings, launched on floods of that new invention, champagne, started with bawdy conversation, went on to obscene songs, and ended in a free-for-all. It was said, quite accurately, that the Regent took a new mistress every week.

The duchesse de Berry did her best to keep up with her father. She soon moved into the Luxembourg Palace and held court there. In the evenings there were great feasts at which the duch-ess, in grand court dress covered with diamonds, would become thoroughly drunk and, more often than not, stagger to the corner of the room and throw up. Her lovers included servants, soldiers, noblemen: vigor was the only requirement. Sometimes she attended her father's suppers: there was the night, for instance, of the great competition when the judgment of Paris was reenacted for her father's pleasure. Mmes de Berry, d'Arverne, and de Parabère stripped naked and impersonated Aphrodite, Athena, and Hera. Of course, Berry-Aphrodite won.

Her debauchery seemed especially outré when this woman who was willing to sleep with anyone, and who could be seen staggering drunkenly every night, also revealed herself as a monster of pride. In all outward particulars the duchess behaved exactly as if she were Queen of France. She held court and demanded respectful attendance; she dressed with great splendor and appropriated the Crown diamonds for her own use. She even exacted marks of honor no Queen had ever received: a full regiment of guards as an escort, for instance.

Her pretensions seemed even more senseless when the duchess fell in love with M. de Rions, an unattractive, pimply young man who had acquired a reputation for unexcelled virility. He first met the duchess when he seduced her Woman of the Bedchamber; soon he was sharing his favors between maid and mistress. In no time, to everyone's amazement, the dragon was conquered: Mme de Berry, unchanged in every other respect, became like putty in Rions's hands. He scolded; she cried. He beat her; she begged his forgiveness. He humiliated her in public; she sobbed and kissed his hands. No one could do anything with her, not even the Regent, who for once appeared really upset.

Soon the affair had become an open scandal. The duchess gave birth to a—luckily—dead baby and still refused to let Rions go. There was, after all, no reason why she should deny herself anything: the system invented by Louis XIV was bearing fruit. Since he had given the King and the royal family a semidivine status, the duchess felt unrestrained by normal rules. And since she had grown accustomed to indulging herself exactly as her father did, there was no reason to give up the man she loved.

Then death once again intervened. Mme de Berry became sick, lingered in great pain for a few weeks, and, having faced her approaching end with dauntless courage, died on July 21, 1719. She was barely twenty-four.

The autopsy revealed what we would call cirrhosis of the liver along with a variety of infections and brain damage, possibly of syphilitic origin. In the streets the people sang:

> Babet has passed away,
> What a loss for Eros!
> What, Babet the actress?
> No, Babet of the Luxembourg.

Except for her father, everyone considered her death a good riddance.

That the duchesse de Berry was ambitious, proud, and debauched is beyond dispute. Why shouldn't she have been? Hers was a world where people would kill for precedence, where to be self-seeking was to be smart, where to be false was to be royal. Wherever she looked, Mme de Berry saw men drinking, philandering, taking pride in the number of women they bedded, and boasting about it. Why shouldn't she?

Once she had achieved marriage to the duc de Berry, there was no challenge left for this brilliant woman: a Granddaughter of France had no place to go. She could try to gather a few more marks of rank; she could cover herself with diamonds. Beyond that, her intelligence and energy must go unused. Then, too, she was always unable to see why her behavior must differ from a man's. If her father could sleep with maids, she could with footmen. If he had orgies, so could she. At the onset of a century when, for the first time, women became as good as men, the duchesse de Berry set a lasting precedent by claiming and enjoying the freedom which had for so long been denied to the supposedly weaker sex.

Had she been less bold, less free, less equal, she might well have lived longer. A little later in the century, she would have had outlets other than drink and promiscuous sex for her talents

and energies. But scandalous though she was, the duchesse de Berry did as much to set a pattern for the eighteenth-century woman as the chaste and powerful Mme des Ursins.

The Sway of Intelligence
Madame du Deffand
Madame de Pompadour

Madame du Deffand, Horace Walpole wrote in his edition of her letters, exemplified "the graces of the most polished style which, however, are less beautiful than the graces of the wit they clothe." Like Mme de Sévigné, whom she so admired, Mme du Deffand deserves to be placed among the ranks of the great letter writers. Yet her real achievement lies elsewhere, for in a century where conversation was the supreme art, she invented the salon.

Marie de Vichy was born in 1696 to a noble but somewhat obscure family whose connections were the very best. She was the granddaughter of the duchesse de Choiseul and the niece of the duchesse de Luynes, and she based her life and salon on the influence of those two powerful relatives. Like all girls of her station, she was sent at the age of seven to an elegant convent, one of those eighteenth-century institutions whose mother superiors were usually better known for their love affairs than their piety. There, much to her anger in later years, she proceeded to learn almost nothing: the social graces, writing, and a little music were considered the material of an adequate curriculum. At the age of twenty-one she returned to society in order to marry the marquis du Deffand. As was almost always the case, her father had arranged the match without consulting her.

Luckily, this was in August, 1718, when the Regent ruled, the duchesse de Berry set the tone, and fidelity was hardly expected of a pretty, sexy, and intelligent bride. It was just as well, for the honeymoon, spent in M. du Deffand's country château, proved a sharp disappointment to the new marquise. The poor man might be good-tempered, athletic, and kind, but he was unbearably dull and made love so badly that the pleasure remained all his.

Through her long life, boredom was always Mme du Deffand's great fear. "What else shall I tell you about myself?" she wrote to Walpole almost fifty years later. "Nothing, except that I am bored to death." In youth, at least, there were ways to combat dullness: the attractive marquise soon found herself one of the ornaments of the duchesse de Berry's court. She attended the Regent's suppers, became his mistress for two weeks, met everyone, and charmed all she met. When men palled, there was conversation; and when that became tiresome, there was gambling.

Everyone at Versailles had gambled, often large sums, and many had cheated. Now, the mania was at its most virulent in the salon of Mme de Mirepoix where, according to Mme du Deffand, "This passion made me lose interest in everything; all I thought about was cards. . . . Finally, I became disgusted and cured myself of that folly." It was no loss: Mme de Mirepoix remained a lifelong friend, and besides, one cannot help feeling that the passion was not all that strong. Still, in her statement Mme du Deffand neatly summed herself up: there was no madness which she could not conquer, nothing she deeply cared about, except, perhaps, conversation.

For the moment, all was well. M. du Deffand knew that his wife was sleeping with half the men in Paris, but he was an agreeable husband and pretended he noticed nothing. Even in this age of general laxity, Mme du Deffand had an extraordinary number of lovers, probably because she cared so little about them. She became known as one of the most abandoned women around— no mean feat, considering the competition. Eventually, after two and a half years of silence, poor M. du Deffand did complain. His wife laughed at him. So, retreating back to that country château, he left her.

While no woman was expected to be faithful to her husband, it was considered scandalous to be altogether separated from him. Discretion might have done wonders for the marquise's social position, but when, following the custom of the 1720s, she chose to announce every new lover by appearing with him in a box at the Opéra, it was noticed that her companions changed almost daily, and she began to find herself snubbed by some of the more respectable duchesses. Still, she had the Regent on her side. After his death in

1723, however, the marquise suddenly found herself very unpopular. Luckily there was one other place where she might just be able to avoid boredom: the fairylike palace of Sceaux.

There, amid lush gardens dotted with sculpture, lived a gay, busy little court centering on an imperious mistress, the duchesse du Maine. "No one could be more unjust, more self-satisfied, and more tyrannical," Président Hénault wrote of her. This tiny woman, born a princess of the blood royal, was married to a dull bastard son of Louis XIV who usually stayed out of sight. In an effort to rectify the error of fate which had cost her husband the throne, she had plotted with the Spanish ambassador and been found out. Now, forbidden Paris and the court, she gathered in her sumptuous château those guests who would come: rich middle-class men on the rise, like Président Hénault; women whose lives had been a little too scandalous, like Mme du Deffand; and intellectuals, a category of people who had yet to be recognized as decent company. All in all, it was a lively group.

There were dances, theatricals, garden fetes, and regattas on the canal. The duchess feared boredom too, and she loved the theater more than anything else in the world. Luckily, Voltaire was always fond of royalty and became a frequent guest; soon other intellectuals followed. It was not a salon yet: conversation was only for empty moments, but it existed. There Mme du Deffand started a lifelong friendship with Voltaire, as well as a singularly tepid affair with Président Hénault. The marquise herself quickly became one of the court's stars. "Nobody has more natural wit. The lively flame that feeds it lights every subject to its very depths, takes it out of itself, and gives the simplest topics great interest. [Mme du Deffand] has, to the supreme degree, a talent for depicting character. Her portraits are more alive than their models, and help one to know them even better than if one were on terms of the greatest intimacy with them," wrote one of Mme du Maine's ladies.

Sceaux was a great help in another way: room, board, and heat in the winter were all free. If he couldn't have his wife, M. du Deffand was at least determined to have her dowry, so in the thirties and forties the marquise had to make do with meager funds. Even with the 3,000-livre pension obtained for her by a friend at court, her yearly income amounted to only 13,000 livres (by this time the livre was worth about $3). It was barely enough to maintain a small apartment, keep two or three servants, and open a salon: for now, in the mid-thirties, Mme du Deffand had invented a new sort of social gathering.

Of course, society had always congregated at court, but there pomp and gossip banished real conversation. A few princes—the duchesse du Maine, the prince de Conti—had daily gatherings where people could be freer than at court, but the intellectual level of the conversation was fairly low. Finally, a few great nobles, such as Mme de Mirepoix, received their peers and provided wonderful food, great wines, and gambling tables; but no one except Mme du Deffand had thought of blending together society people and intellectuals, marshals of France and pretty women, ministers of state and foreigners, all on an equal footing. As it turned out, the marquise was uniquely suited to do this. By the thirties her scandalous behavior was safely past. She had only one lover, Président Hénault, who was there so often that he had become as respectable as a husband. Besides, he was a social climber who made himself pleasant to everyone, behaved in the most conventional way, and soon actually managed to become a member of the Queen's little circle. Since Mme du Deffand was as pretty, bright, and amusing as ever, her grand relations resumed visiting her and brought their fellow courtiers, including that irresistible seducer, that quintessence of eighteenth-century man, the duc de Richelieu.

The duke was a great-grand-nephew of the famous cardinal de Richelieu, the seventeenth-century prime minister. He had inherited not only the name, the dukedom, and a substantial fortune, but also the position of First Gentleman of the Bedchamber to the King, one of the most important at court. He was polished, racy, amusing—an eighteenth-century Don Juan whom no woman could resist. He was also a competent soldier. Unlike most dukes, he valued intelligence

and counted Voltaire among his friends. Richelieu should have been the happiest man in Paris; instead, he suffered from two radical disabilities. First, he was ambitious and dreamed of emulating his ancestor the cardinal, but he was so obviously frivolous and greedy that the King, whom he amused, kept him firmly away from power. Second, he felt humiliated by the fact that, while he was descended from the great cardinal in the female line, his grandfather had never been more than a country squire. So he thirsted for honors: the Saint-Esprit, that French equivalent of the Garter, and the august title of marshal of France.

With all that, the duke was the best of company and a wonderful recruit for Mme du Deffand's salon. In addition to amusing aristocrats, the marquise could draw on other new acquaintances: Hénault, of course, who was both witty and charming; Voltaire, incomparably brilliant, as always; Montesquieu, sound, enlightening, eloquent, whose L'Esprit des Lois was a major influence on the American Founding Fathers; then, soon, d'Alembert, Diderot, Marmontel, the creators of the Enlightenment, whose names echoed throughout Europe and made French the only civilized language. And there were also the beauties of the day: Mme de Vintimille, for instance, who was the King's mistress and who regularly came to glean the latest witticisms for his amusement.

It was all very new, especially since there was nothing splendid about Mme du Deffand's parties. She lived in a small, plainly decorated apartment; her suppers were notoriously bad; there were no entertainments, no balls, no masquerades. Clearly you did not need money to create a salon; you simply had to know how to blend people, lead the conversation, and make everyone shine. The talk was free, lively, pleasing. You could discuss any subject as long as you made it interesting, but no one was allowed to hold forth. Reciprocity was everything. There was no doctrine to be defended, no point of view to be imposed, no sacred cow to be defended; only dullness was forbidden. As for the topics, they ranged from the latest news to the latest books, from court gossip to current plays, from politics to philosophy.

This new formula was greeted with enthusi-

Sèvres porcelain potpourri vase. This vase, purchased by Mme de Pompadour,
is one of the finest products of the Sèvres porcelain factory which she
sponsored and patronized. The Metropolitan Museum of Art, New York.
Gift of Samuel H. Kress Foundation, 1958 (58.75.88)

asm; soon Mme du Deffand became known all
through Europe. Foreigners arriving in Paris
begged for an introduction, and the French
flocked to her with more eagerness still. The marquise had invented the social form most representative of her culture and century. Conversation,
that specifically French achievement which, later
in the century, Mme de Staël called an art in
itself, was perfected in Mme du Deffand's salon.

Soon rivals began to appear, but it was to the
marquise's parties that the best, most interesting
people came year after year.

It was just as well, really; how else could she
have kept boredom at bay, how else survived her
deep cynicism? "Whenever you confide your sor-
rows to anyone, you provide them with a nasty
sort of enjoyment and abase yourself in their eyes,"
she wrote. In truth, amid a world of acquaint-

Carmontelle. *Mme du Deffand.*
Collection Paul Oulmont,
Musée Départemental des Vosges, Epinal, France

Boucher. *The Breakfast.* This is the kind of house that
Mme de Pompadour lived in before she moved to Versailles.
The Metropolitan Museum of Art, New York.
The Elisha Whittelsey Collection, The Elisha Whittelsey Fund,
1950 (50.567.34)

ances, she never had a friend.

Perhaps it was because she knew herself so little. This is how she described herself in 1728: "Mme la marquise du Deffand is the enemy of anything fake or affected, her speech and her face are always the faithful interpreters of the feelings in her soul." By 1768 her characterization of herself had changed: "Mme de . . . is so very artificial that no one could guess what she would be like if she allowed herself to be seen as she really is." Almost forty years had passed, of course, but the marquise had hardly altered; both portraits are equally untrue. On a shrewder note, she added: "Often she falls into a boredom which puts out all the lights in her mind; that condition is unbearable to her, and makes her so unhappy that she throws herself blindly on any deliverance; hence the fickleness of her words and the imprudence of her behavior." Nothing could better describe this bored, cold, and curiously heartless woman.

The marquise seemed unchangeable, but around 1750 she began to surprise herself. M. du Deffand died, so she recovered her dowry. Finding herself more prosperous, she moved to a new, larger, more splendid apartment, which she decorated with great care. Soon the luxury and excellence of her suppers became famous. Curiously, instead of being elated, she sank into a deep depression. Président Hénault was no help: the Queen found him amusing, so he was spending most of his time at Versailles. Even d'Alembert, whose conversation usually enthralled the marquise, failed to cheer her. Most uncharacteristically, she decided that she would spend some time with her brother at his château in Burgundy.

For a while it seemed that the warmth of family life was working a cure. In reality, Mme du Deffand had come across a brilliant young woman, Julie de Lespinasse, whose sparkling conversation and lively enthusiasm revived the jaded Parisienne. Soon it became obvious that this pearl wanted to leave home. Mlle de Lespinasse was the illegitimate daughter of M. de Vichy, the marquise's brother, and his mother-in-law—an awkward relative if ever there was one. Rashly, the marquise invited Julie to move in with her.

When she was informed of the pending event, the duchesse de Luynes prudently wrote the marquise that while Mlle de Lespinasse was no doubt perfect in every way, people usually tired of these live-in dependents and eventually grew to hate them. Mme du Deffand saw her point: Julie was given her own little three-room apartment just below the marquise's. In no time she had become indispensable. Mme du Deffand, who had been having trouble with her eyes, began to go blind; and Julie read all the new books aloud to her. Then, too, the new companion was bright, amusing, and a fast learner. She soon held her own in Mme du Deffand's salon, and the men liked her all the better for being young and pretty. It was an ideal arrangement.

Just at this time in the 1750s, the world began to change. Many intellectuals began to attack abuses of church and state. The brilliant d'Alembert, who had become closer than ever to the marquise, launched the great project of his life, the *Encyclopédie.* This compendium of all knowledge marked one of the milestones in the development of the human mind. It was also clearheaded—or disrespectful, depending on how you chose to look at it—when it came to defining miracles, for instance, or the nature of taxation. Now, for all her sarcasm, the marquise was very much a member of the Establishment. She might be irreligious herself, but she thought that believing in God and the divinity of Jesus would probably be a great comfort, so she didn't at all like the new tone adopted by the intellectuals. Then, greatly to her annoyance, a rival salon opened its doors. Soon Mme Geoffrin was gathering in all the *Encyclopédistes,* along with playwrights and artists. At least this threat was bearable, because Mme Geoffrin was a mere bourgeoise and therefore contemptible. Besides, her class made it impossible for her to attract the brilliant aristocratic crowd so prized by Mme du Deffand.

Then her world fell apart. As she aged, Mme du Deffand found it increasingly difficult to sleep at night, so she asked her guests to come a little later than before. Since they had grown to like Mlle de Lespinasse, however, they simply stopped in her little apartment for an hour or two before going upstairs. The marquise eventually discovered what they were doing and, because her salon was the whole world to her, bitterly reproached Julie for her treachery. The companion retaliated with a vivid and unpleasant description of the old lady's tyranny. The scene lasted for a whole day and ended when Julie, who had been thrown out, took refuge at the house of Mme Geoffrin, thus adding insult to injury. Worse, she soon opened her own salon, starring none other than d'Alembert. It almost broke the marquise's heart.

Now her salon began to seem stale. Conversation, Mme du Deffand complained, had become cold and dull. The older people had run out of things to say, and the younger ones were simply not civilized. Mlle de Lespinasse was replaced by Wiart, the most faithful of secretaries, but it wasn't the same.

Still, the pattern was set: the blind old lady, sitting in her deep armchair near the fireplace with her faithful and notoriously wicked dog on her lap, talked, listened, went in to sumptuous suppers with her guests, and, when she was left alone, stayed up most of the night beset by insomnia. Now that the great storm provoked by Mlle de Lespinasse had subsided, nothing was ever going to change.

And then at the age of sixty-eight, for the first time in her life, the marquise fell in love. "You could not be loved more tenderly than I love you," she wrote. And again: "Only loving matters. People who don't love . . . can never find real happiness."

Unfortunately her passion was not shared, for although Horace Walpole was bright, witty, and fond of chat, he was also terrified of ridicule. At first when he was taken to Mme du Deffand's salon during one of those trips to Paris which tore him away from his beloved Strawberry Hill, he thought he had found heaven itself. As for the blind marquise, she had at last met someone who was lively, entertaining, wellborn (his father was Robert Walpole, Earl of Oxford, the great Prime Minister), someone with whom she had everything in common, someone she could and did love: it was a revolution; but Walpole, who was almost twenty years younger, was quite as cold as

Mme du Deffand had once been, and while it was flattering to become the star of the most famous salon in Paris, he could imagine the snickering if his noble friends found out that Mme du Deffand was in love with him.

Of course, the marquise was too smart not to catch on. She quickly explained that when she said love, she meant friendship, and promised to control herself; but the real feeling kept slipping out. "What cowardice, what weakness I have been displaying! I had promised myself I wouldn't, but, but. . . . Forget all that, and forgive me, my tutor," she wrote him soon after he left Paris, for he became her "tutor," and she styled herself his "pupil."

There is no doubt that within his limitations, Walpole was enormously fond of Mme du Deffand. For one thing, they were really very much alike. For another, he was safely ensconced in his own house across the English Channel except for a month or two every few years, and he loved her vivid, entertaining letters, full of the latest news and court gossip. Finally, he was a thorough snob, and the marquise not only knew everyone, but was especially close to the Choiseuls. As it happened, the duc de Choiseul was both prime minister and the most fashionable man in France.

Of course, for all her newfound emotion, Mme du Deffand continued to see the world precisely as she had before. "I am just like the late Regent," she wrote Walpole in 1766. "Everybody I see seems either stupid or dishonest; all the judgments I hear people making are unbearable to me." Nor did she become less cold to others. "M. le duc de Chevreuse [the son of her aunt, the duchesse de Luynes] is seriously ill, they tell me he's melting away like so much hot wax. Adieu, I'm going to eat some Bavarian cream," she wrote a year later.

In fact, once again the world was becoming dull. "I esteem no one," she wrote, "and yet cannot do without those people for whom I feel contempt." This time, however, the marquise's grey mood had some basis in fact. Her salon, glamorous as ever, had become distinctly more specialized. Most of the intellectuals were gone; so were the artists. Only the courtiers remained, and one by one, her old friends were dying. In 1770 Choiseul was disgraced and exiled to his château at Chanteloup; to our great good luck, her conversations with him became purely epistolary. Even when his exile ended four years later, things somehow weren't the same. Everyone was becoming difficult. Voltaire and the Choiseuls quarreled; Walpole was so nasty at one point that the marquise's relationship with him was almost broken off. And the new people just weren't up to snuff. Although the marquise quite liked M. and Mme Necker, especially after he became minister of finance, she found him often pompous and dull; besides, their salon was almost entirely political.

So she went out, and received people, more busily than ever: at least it filled her time. Every night Wiart read to her until daybreak, but still the hours dragged. "The only misfortune in life is to be born. I find there is not a single way of life, of any kind whatever, that is preferable to nothingness," she had written to Voltaire. At long last, on September 23, 1780, the misfortune of being alive ceased for her. Free now from the fear of ridicule, Walpole was finally able to do his friend justice. By publishing her letters, he made sure that long after the reputation of her salon had faded, Mme du Deffand would be remembered gratefully by all those who find pleasure in a lively mind and a sharp pen.

Madame de Pompadour

It didn't mean much to be the Regent's mistress: the troop of these ladies was large and their influence nonexistent, as Mme du Deffand could have testified; but to become the King's official mistress was very different. Louis XIV codified the etiquette regarding mistresses in the great days of Mmes de La Vallière and de Montespan, and it lasted unchanged until the Revolution. Foremost among the powerful offices of state was that of the royal mistress. It entailed a number of perquisites: money, jewelry, precedence—that life-blood of the court—and of course, enormous fame. The lady's son or husband was likely to be made a duke (as were the ducs d'Antin, de La Vallière, and de Rohan-Soubise, among others), her younger son or nephew a cardinal. The nicest thing of all was that, really, there was no dishonor involved if your wife or mother was the mistress. In France the King had actually become semidivine. It was rather like Zeus and his innumerable women: you didn't refuse a god.

All those good things, however, came only to the *maîtresse déclarée*. The King was expected to have countless little affairs, lasting a day, a week, even a month, with middle- or lower-class women. Each might be given a few thousand livres, but obviously there was no question of a role at court. So when, in 1745, people realized that Louis XV was seeing the pretty Madame d'Etioles, no one paid much attention. "All the masquerade balls have given rise to talk about the King's new love . . . , a Mme d'Etioles who is young and pretty. . . . If the fact is true, it will probably be a passing affair and not a mistress," the duc de Luynes, a well-informed courtier, wrote in his diary. He could not have been more wrong.

Mme d'Etioles was a typical product of the new enriched bourgeoisie. Her parents, named Poisson (Fish—later the subject of endless puns), belonged to a network of rich speculators and *fermiers-généraux.** She had been married, at the usual age of twenty, to M. Lenormant d'Etioles, a nephew of her mother's lover and a *fermier-général* himself. Naturally there could be no question of presenting her at court, since her family would need to prove that it had been noble since the year 1400. Anyway, she didn't even know anyone there.

People she did know—well-to-do Parisians of no particular social standing—all found her exceptional. She was enormously pretty, bright, and funny. In a day when the haute couture had not yet been invented, and women designed their own clothes with the help of a dressmaker, she was extraordinarily elegant. She had a feeling for decoration, too: everybody loved her château at Etioles. She understood food; she could sing, dance, play

Lemoyne. *Louis XV.* The Metropolitan Museum of Art, New York. Gift of George Blumenthal, 1941 (41.100.244)

---

*Taxes were collected by the *fermiers-généraux* all through the ancien régime. They undertook every year to pay the treasury a certain sum, then saw to it that they collected a good deal more than they had to pay out. "As rich as a *fermier-général,*" people said.

the harpsichord, even act. Altogether, she was enchanting.

It is hard to say just what she looked like. She was tall, svelte, graceful, with an oval face, light brown hair, and perfect teeth, a rarity in an age without dentists. Evidently she had a dazzling smile and magnetic, sparkling eyes, but none of her portraits looks quite like any other. She was, it seems, one of those women whose particular attraction shines out in the give-and-take of relationships, whose charm is overwhelming but cannot be put on canvas. Evidently it worked even at a distance: when she began to follow the King's hunt in the forest near Etioles (one day she wore a blue dress and drove a pink open carriage, the next day a pink dress and a blue carriage), she was quickly noticed by the King. Nothing happened, though; Mme de Chateauroux, the *maîtresse déclarée,* saw to that.

Then on December 8, 1744, Mme de Chateauroux was dead, and within the week, young Mme d'Etioles met the King. At first she was led in secret to Louis XV's private apartments. It was all very discreet; M. d'Etioles was sent away on a business trip by his uncle; Mme d'Etioles came and went in the dead of night; the duc de Luynes's notion that she was a passing fancy seemed accurate. Only, the King loved to dance, and Mme d'Etioles was a wonderful dancer. During the month-long festivities, including many costume balls, that accompanied the marriage of the Dauphin, an unmistakably commanding figure was seen to dance again and again with Mme d'Etioles.

Tongues wagged, but people began wondering if the King was seriously in love only after the masked ball in the great Hall of Mirrors at Versailles on February 27, 1745. Even after the Queen, dressed as a shepherdess but wearing huge diamonds, had come out with the rest of the royal family, the King failed to appear. Then a side door opened and eight men walked in wearing identical costumes which made them look just like the topiary yew trees in the park outside. It was obvious that one of the walking bushes was the King. The seven who were not soon found themselves making successful love to pretty Pari-

Overleaf: Cochin. *The Yew Tree Ball.* This is the famous ball at which Mme de Pompadour's liaison with the King became obvious. The King and his attendants, disguised as topiary yew trees, can be seen on the right. The Queen, dressed as a shepherdess, is in the center. The Metropolitan Museum of Art, New York. The Elisha Whittelsey Collection, The Elisha Whittelsey Fund, 1930 (30.22 (34/34))

Pigalle. *Mme de Pompadour.*
The Metropolitan Museum of Art, New York.
The Jules Bache Collection, 1949 (49.7.70)

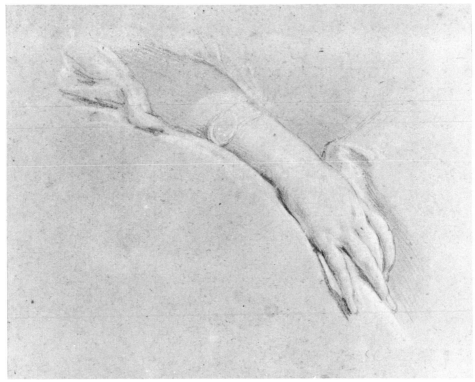

Boucher. *Study for the left hand of Mme de Pompadour.* The Metropolitan
Museum of Art, New York. Rogers Fund, 1955 (55.214)

sians who hoped that they had snared the monarch. As for Louis XV, who unmasked after a short while, he was seen disappearing with Mme d'Etioles.

Shortly afterward, the King went off to war. Mme d'Etioles settled in her country château and proceeded to enjoy a summer made livelier by the electric presence of Voltaire, and happier by the daily arrival of letters from the front. Then one day the address on the letters changed: instead of *A Madame d'Etioles,* it read *A Madame la marquise de Pompadour.* Within were the letters-patent establishing the marquessate, as well as the title deed to an estate. And when the campaign ended, a royal carriage drew up to a side door in Versailles. Out came a ravishing young woman who moved into a suite of rooms just above the King's own. Mme de Pompadour was about to become the official mistress.

Of course, there was an explosion of hatred and disappointment. One of those awful little bourgeoises was snatching an envied position from under the noses of the titled ladies at court. It was a dreadful blow to the aristocratic pride

of everyone at Versailles: imagine having to kowtow to someone who wasn't even *born!** The consolation was that ridicule would kill her in no time. After all, the customs of the court, *ce pays-ci* ("this country," as it was called), were complex and altogether different from those of the rest of the world. There were special ways to talk, to walk, to curtsy, and the little Fish wouldn't know any of them.

But she did; she had been learning them throughout the summer at Etioles. On the great day of her presentation at court, she was seen, maddeningly, to glide, curtsy, and kick back her train as if to the manner born.

Soon it was obvious to everyone that the King and the new marquise were very much in love. It wasn't just that they spent their nights together: they talked, they walked, they laughed, they obviously enjoyed each other's company. By October, 1745, habits which were to last for

———————

*Only the nobles were said to be *born*—a contraction of wellborn.

twenty years had been set. The duc de Luynes wrote:

> As soon as the King is dressed, he goes down to Mme de Pompadour's; he stays with her until he goes to mass; after mass, he goes back to her and eats soup and a chop, for His Majesty does not have a real dinner.* [When he isn't hunting] he stays there until five or six, when he attends to business. On Council days, he visits her before and after. Everybody tells me they find Mme de Pompadour extremely polite. She is not nasty, she doesn't say unpleasant things about people [practically everybody else at court did], she doesn't even allow other people to do so. She is cheerful and likes to talk. Far from being proud, she continually refers to her family in the King's presence.

The new mistress was proving to be a rare bird indeed. She was nice to the Queen and saw to it that the King paid his consort some attention, settled her debts, and gave her presents. Instead of proving her power by having her enemies exiled from court, Mme de Pompadour tried to win them over. The duc de Richelieu is a case in point. When he wasn't shining in Mme du Deffand's salon and seducing every woman in sight, he was plotting to become a marshal of France and prime minister. The way to achieve his goals seemed clear enough: if he could furnish the King with a mistress, then she would see to it that he got what he wanted. He loathed the middle-class intruder who had stolen the position.

Richelieu, being so touchy about his grandfather's humble status, was a terrific snob, more prejudiced than the most reactionary of the other dukes. He objected to Mme de Pompadour on two counts: by advancing her own friends, she would keep him down; and, horror of horrors, as a bourgeoise she was intruding into the court's sacred precincts. He proceeded to make her life as unpleasant as possible by being unfailingly rude and critical. Since he amused the King and was his frequent companion, the duke's nuisance value was considerable. Any other mistress would have had him sent off to his estate near Bordeaux; Mme de Pompadour, on the other hand, kept trying to win him over. A few years later, he led

*That is, lunch. Our dinner was called a *souper*.

his army to victory and was indeed made a marshal of France, thus achieving at least one of his ambitions. The lady not only forbore to interfere with the promotion, but even congratulated him.

"Sincère et tendre Pompadour" ("sincere and tender Pompadour"), Voltaire called her, and he was right. She didn't lie, she didn't conceal, she didn't hate. She was, it seems, genuinely kind and full of good will. Then too, she really loved the King for himself. Power, position, money, all were secondary; it was keeping Louis XV's love which mattered to her. She did that by being intelligent, cultivated, curious. Best of all, she knew how to enjoy life and managed to amuse this most bored of monarchs.

Until he met the marquise, the King's only hobbies had been hunting and sex; she introduced him to the arts. She was friendly with Voltaire

Van Loo. *The Pretty Gardener.* This is a portrait of Mme de Pompadour. The Metropolitan Museum of Art, New York. Purchase, Roland L. Redmond Gift, Louis V. Bell and Rogers Funds, 1972 (1972.539.22)

Boucher. *The Toilet of Venus.* Mme de Pompadour ordered this painting from Boucher
for one of the rooms in her château at Bellevue. The Metropolitan Museum of Art,
New York. Bequest of William K. Vanderbilt, 1920 (20.155.9)

and understood writers, and now she encouraged, protected, and subsidized them. Voltaire himself became historiographer of France and, even more to his taste, a Gentleman-in-Ordinary. When the great *Encyclopédie* was banned for being disrespectful to the powers-that-be, Mme de Pompadour devised a simple stratagem that led the King to lift the ban. One evening she and a few others were having supper with Louis XV at Trianon. The conversation having turned to the hunt, the duc de La Vallière asked if anyone knew how gunpowder was made—or, for that matter, face powder. No one did. "Well, Sire," the marquise said, "if only we could have the *Encyclopédie,* it would answer all our questions." Ban or no ban, the King owned the already published volumes. He sent for them and, having learned how gunpowder is made, allowed publication to resume.

Then there was the theater. The marquise had a passion for private theatricals, and she herself was a first-class actress—better, indeed, than many professionals. She set up a little private theater in Versailles where only the King and a few carefully chosen guests were admitted. It was a huge success; all the spectators enjoyed themselves, the actors did too, Mme de Pompadour shone, and the lucky authors whose plays were performed usually went home with a pension. Of course, the duc de Richelieu, resentful as ever, tried to ruin everything. As First Gentleman of the Bedchamber, he had jurisdiction over the Menus Plaisirs, the department in charge of all the King's entertainment. On being told one day that the marquise had requested certain sets and costumes, he flatly refused to let them go. This time the victim spoke up. In the afternoon as Richelieu was pulling off the King's boots after the hunt, his sovereign asked him how many times he had been imprisoned in the Bastille, so far. "Three times, Sire," the duke answered. Within minutes the sets were on their way.

Mme de Pompadour's enlightened patronage extended to painters and sculptors as well. She was, of course, painted innumerable times by the great artists of the period—Boucher, La Tour, Van Loo, and others. She also commissioned work from them and paid them punctually. Among the

French art from the mid-eighteenth century that is seen in museums today, a significant portion of the best pieces once belonged to her. *The Toilet of Venus* by Boucher, at The Metropolitan Museum of Art in New York, is a case in point. The marquise so loved the visual arts, in fact, that she made engravings herself and even had a printing press transferred one day from the Imprimerie Royale to her apartment at Versailles. There a new edition of Corneille's *Rodogune* was struck off as she watched. Its title page bears the words *Au Nord*—Mme de Pompadour's apartment was in the north wing of the palace—and it is adorned with a Pompadour engraving.

Most important of all, perhaps, the favorite loved to build and decorate houses, and the King soon shared that taste. Some of the buildings were tiny—the Hermitage at Versailles was a little one-floor pavilion thirty-six by thirty-six feet—and some were quite grand, as at Bellevue or Choisy; but everywhere the decorative arts shone at their unexcelled best. Today we tend to think of decoration as a convenience or a frivolity; but the French in the eighteenth century produced furniture, porcelain, bronzes, and wall paneling so beautiful to look at, so exquisitely crafted that they became a major form of art. Nor were painters afraid of cooperating: the greatest artists—Fragonard, Boucher, Van Loo—painted panels that were carefully planned to fit over a door or into a boiserie. Most of Mme de Pompadour's houses were destroyed during the Revolution, but we can still see some of her rooms at Versailles itself. The paneling, the floors, the mirrors are still there, but the admirable profusion of inlaid furniture and precious silks, of vases and clocks and objects, the great masses of hothouse flowers—these are gone. We can only imagine them as we walk through the empty rooms.

It was lucky, too, that the marquise had a brother, M. de Marigny, who understood and loved the arts. He was soon made Superintendent of the King's Buildings, a post in which he was able to protect and stimulate the current artistic explosion. It is owing to him that the great Jacques Ange Gabriel was able to build the Ecole Militaire and the two palaces on the Place de la

Concorde in Paris, as well as that most beautiful of houses, that simple but perfect jewel, the Petit Trianon.

Earlier favorites had wanted titles and money, but Mme de Pompadour cared more about making the King happy than anything else. Of course she had diamonds—she could hardly have appeared at Versailles without them—but far more important, she created the kind of luxurious, beautiful environment which, like the salon, was one of the discoveries of eighteenth-century France. Magnificently carved boiseries had to be specially ordered for all those new rooms, those new châteaus, along with inlaid furniture, new carpets, curtains, mirrors, and paintings. The marquise loved planning and ordering it all, and so did the King.

Of course, people complained about the expense and said that the greedy favorite was bleeding France white. Luckily we have accounts: during her last eighteen years as the King's mistress, the marquise received a total of some 37 million livres (about $110 million), or just over 2 million livres a year at a time when the treasury receipts averaged 300 million. Of the sums she received, a significant amount went into building and decorating. But since, with the single exception of Ménars, all the marquise's houses were built on royal land, they reverted to the King at her death. In fact, her personal property was probably worth a little less than 2 million livres.

It was normal for a favorite to be denounced as expensive. Since the tax system was unfair, oppressive, and inefficient, but had not yet been recognized as such, it was comfortable to have a highly visible person to blame. Soon, however, the public had a new complaint about the marquise. While the favorite had always had a good deal to say about court appointments, she was not supposed to meddle in politics. The King ruled alone; his ministers were there only to carry out his orders (although they provided convenient scapegoats when things went wrong), and the mistress was supposedly outside the circuit. Now Mme de Pompadour was being consulted in affairs of state; worse, she was acting as a surrogate foreign minister.

Corneille's "Rodogune." Right, title page of the edition that was printed in Mme de Pompadour's apartment in the north wing (Au Nord) of the palace of Versailles; *left,* frontispiece engraved by Mme de Pompadour from a design by Boucher. The Pierpont Morgan Library, New York

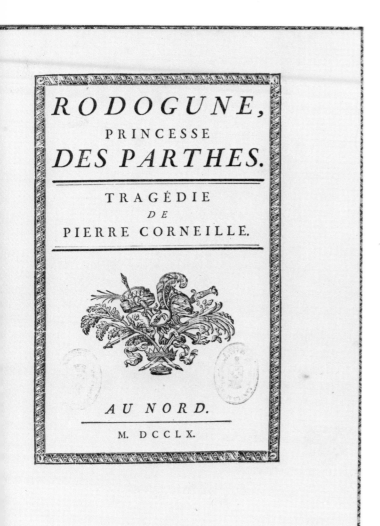

RODOGUNE,
PRINCESSE
DES PARTHES.

TRAGÉDIE
DE
PIERRE CORNEILLE.

AU NORD.

M. DCCLX.

Little by little, Louis XV transformed his mistress into the equivalent of a U.S. presidential assistant for national security affairs. He talked to her at length and listened to her comments. He used her as a conduit through which generals or ministers could be told things that the King preferred not to say directly. He consulted her on most major appointments. Finally, he entrusted her as his agent in the great reversal of alliances, when France switched from Prussia to Austria, because negotiations had to be conducted in absolute secrecy, and no one else could be trusted not to leak information.

This was all the more surprising in that sometime in 1752, Mme de Pompadour stopped being the King's mistress. She had always found sex exhausting and not altogether pleasant, but from love for the King, and fear that he would take another mistress, she tried to spur herself on. She ate quantities of truffles and vanilla, both of which were considered aphrodisiacs, but instead of becoming passionate, she simply made herself sick. Louis XV had the Bourbon appetite for sex, and for a while the poor marquise was dreadfully worried. Then, slowly, it became plain that the King loved her not as a sex object, but as a stimulating companion, as an intelligent woman whose advice and discretion he could trust—in fact as the very best of friends. However, since he was not about to give up sex, he rented a little house in the Parc-aux-Cerfs area of Versailles, where a series of pretty young girls, one at a time, provided him with a personal brothel. Each usually stayed a year or so, then was found a husband and given a pension. It was a sensible arrangement and worked admirably.

Had the marquise been less clever, she would have tried to conceal the fact that she was no longer the King's mistress; but in a stroke of genius she announced it to everyone. The Queen had always been kind to her; now Mme de Pompadour became a supernumerary lady-in-waiting and the King made her a duchess. In one move she had gained absolute respectability. Even better, her hold on Louis XV no longer depended on the vagaries of sexual caprice. Her position had became unassailable, all the more because the

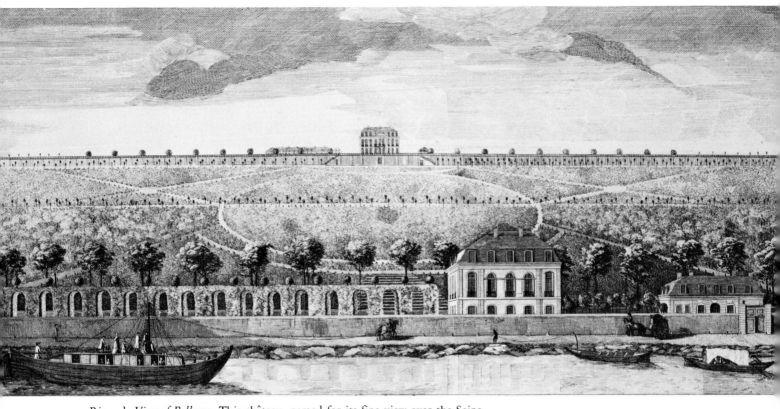

Rigaud. *View of Bellevue.* This château, named for its fine view over the Seine, was one of Mme de Pompadour's favorite retreats. The Metropolitan Museum of Art, New York. Harris Brisbane Dick Fund, 1953 (53.600)

King disliked change and new faces.

Even so, her life was exhausting. Every day great crowds of courtiers attended her to beg for place and favor. "The life I lead is terrible," she wrote her friend Mme de Lutzelbourg. "I hardly have a minute to myself: rehearsals twice a week; continual trips to either the Petit-Château or La Muette, etc. Considerable and unavoidable duties: Queen, Dauphin, Dauphine, who luckily spends the days on her chaise longue [she was pregnant], three daughters [the King's, not hers], two infantas, just see if I can find the time to breathe."

That was in 1749. By 1755, in addition to these duties, she also did the work of a clandestine prime minister. Sitting at her toilette every morning, she listened to officials and solicitors. The King felt that she had less of an ax to grind than most of the ministers, who were after all trying to advance their faction. She was, besides, absolutely honest. More and more, he took to consulting her on appointments and showing her

the state papers. With two exceptions—her recommendations of the abbé de Bernis and the maréchal de Soubise—her advice was excellent. In 1758 she even provided Louis XV with the duc de Choiseul, who turned out to be in many ways the best minister of the reign.

Just how effective the marquise could be is made clear by an unfriendly witness. Durey de Ménières was a member of the Parlement at a time when that body was misbehaving even more than usual. Since it would not do for the King to see him, he was called to Mme de Pompadour's apartment. There, he writes, "alone near the fireplace, she looked me up and down with a hauteur which will remain vivid for the rest of my life, her head inclined toward her shoulder, without even a curtsy, and measuring me in the most imposing way. . . . I was dazzled at the fluency of her speech and the appositeness of its form."

In 1756 the King chose her as his negotiator with Austria. Traditionally France and Prussia had been allied against Austria, England, and Holland; but in 1755–56 Frederick the Great signed a treaty with England, thus leaving France isolated. It was plain that, while Prussia and England were rapacious powers, Austria and France only wanted to maintain the status quo. Still, at Versailles almost everybody was blindly anti-Austrian. When Kaunitz, Maria Theresa's ambassador to France, was instructed to make discreet overtures about a possible alliance, he was told to ignore the ministers, who would have scuttled the project, and speak to the marquise. And it was at her house that Kaunitz met with the King and the abbé de Bernis.

When the negotiations proceeded to a more open and official stage, everyone—especially the bypassed ministers—blamed Mme de Pompadour for bamboozling the King into this foolish new alliance. It is quite true that if the favorite had been rabidly pro-Prussian, she would not have provided Kaunitz with aid and assistance. Nor would he have written: "Everything which has been accomplished by our two courts so far is entirely due, Madame, to your zeal and your wisdom." Then too, the abbé de Bernis, who soon became a minister and proved altogether unequal to his new responsibilites, was entirely the marquise's creature. Still, it was Louis XV who decided on the new policy. The marquise backed it not from conviction but because of her desire to serve the King in any way she could. The King had long been conducting a secret, parallel diplomacy with the aid of the prince de Conti and the comte de Broglie. In using Mme de Pompadour to ensure the secrecy of the negotiations, he treated her once again as an executive assistant rather than a policy maker.

Still, no one understood that. The year 1757, apparently the time of the favorite's greatest triumphs, also marked the height of her unpopularity. On January 5, there was the attempt of the madman Robert Damiens against the King's life. For a few days it seemed as if the marquise might be sent away, but the King went back to her so wholeheartedly that she was able to demand and obtain the dismissal of the war minister Voyer d'Argenson, an old enemy and an

ineffective administrator. Unfortunately, she suggested as his replacement the abbé de Bernis, surely the most unwarlike creature on the face of the earth.* The King agreed, but Bernis didn't last long; within a year he was begging to be allowed to resign. As the Seven Years' War opened, the marquise insisted on the appointment of the maréchal de Soubise as one of the new army commanders. She repented at leisure: the battle of Rossbach turned out to be one of the worst defeats ever suffered by a French army. Of course, it is only fair to add that Soubise's opponent was Frederick the Great and that the maréchal de Richelieu, who thought he should have had Soubise's command, carefully arrived with his troops *after* the battle; still, it didn't look good.

Like other intelligent people, however, the marquise learned from her mistakes. Bernis was dismissed and replaced by the duc de Choiseul who, until 1769, was unquestionably a great minister. He reorganized the army and the treasury, found France allies in Spain, Italy, and southern Germany, and negotiated the Peace of Paris in 1763. This treaty, in which France lost most of its American colonies, was pilloried in the late nineteenth century. At the time, however, it was well received ("What do a few acres of snow matter?" Voltaire said, rightly, about the cession of Canada). But Choiseul, who knew that the French navy had proved sadly lacking, started building ships, improving port facilities, and training naval officers. Just how successful his program had been became apparent when the Thirteen Colonies rebelled and France was able to give them effective help.

With the Choiseul ministry, the marquise felt able to take a less active part in government. The duke consulted her, especially about appointments, but she reverted in part to an earlier role, that of the King's companion, entertainer, and friend. It was already too late, though. She had always been frail, and she never quite recovered

---

*His real talent was for writing light verse. Because of his frivolity, Voltaire had nicknamed him Babet la Bouquetière, Babet the Flower Girl.

Van Loo. *The Trusted Friend.* This painting is a portrait of Mme de Pompadour
in oriental dress. According to her brother, it is the best likeness of her ever painted.
Collection of the Musée des Arts Décoratifs, Paris

from her exertions of the mid-fifties. By 1763 her
heart was beginning to fail. She tried to save her
strength—a hand-cranked elevator lifted her to
her apartment—but life at Versailles remained
impossibly tiring. It wasn't just that the King
must be kept amused, though this in itself was
a full-time job, but there were endless court func-
tions to attend. The solicitors who crowded her
antechamber must be received. Then there were
the usual court intrigues which must be coun-
tered. Altogether, it was more than she could
manage.

With absolute bravery she hid all distressing
symptoms of her deteriorating health from the
King, but death overtook her on April 15, 1764.
She was the only royal mistress to have died in
favor.

Louis XV, supposedly so cold, so uncaring,
collapsed, hiding in his rooms and sobbing. Etiquette forbade his openly mourning the friend he
had loved so deeply. Nor could her body even remain an hour within the palace. That evening the
King was observed by his valet as he stood, bare-
headed in the rain, on the balcony of his bedroom
overlooking the *cour de marbre.* Downstairs a door
opened. Two men carrying a stretcher emerged
hurriedly and placed it in a waiting carriage,
which clattered away as the tears streamed down
the King's face. The marquise-duchesse de Pompadour, *maîtresse déclarée* to the last, was finally
going back to Paris.

3

Writer and Publicist
Betje Wolff
Madame Necker

Life in the quiet, prosperous little Dutch town of Vlissingen was in sharp contrast to the pomp and glamour of Versailles. The Netherlands was an aristocratic republic, governed by their lordships the States-General, a body composed of carefully chosen rich men whose main business was to ensure that the country grew ever richer. Untypically for the century, the idea was not to spend money once you had it, but to reinvest it and grow richer still. Display was frowned upon in this intensely Calvinist atmosphere. While financially the Netherlands was a great power—and an ungenerous one, as Benjamin Franklin was to discover—culturally it had sunk to a low level. The great age of painting was over, and the arts were generally ignored.

It was in Amsterdam and The Hague, however, that many of the great books of the age were printed. This was not just because Dutch printers produced a clear impression on paper of good quality, but because, in foreign languages at least, there was no censorship. It was another money-making stratagem by their lordships. The good burghers were not corrupted by Voltaire's *Candide* or Rousseau's *Nouvelle Héloïse,* since few of them read French. Thus the printing trades grew fat on all the business lost by less tolerant states. That so few people read French is also a commentary on the cultural atmosphere of the Netherlands. In a century when French was the universal language (Frederick the Great barely spoke German, or the Russian court Russian), hardly anyone in Holland spoke anything but Dutch.

Nor was there, as in the rest of Europe, an aristocracy of birth. Money, and only money, mattered. The noblest occupations were those of merchant and banker, since they were also the most remunerative. Safely separated from France by the barrier of the Austrian Netherlands (today's Belgium), the Dutch lived quietly in shining-clean but modest houses. And the strictest kind of morality, it was well understood, must always prevail.

L. Portmann. *Elisabeth Wolff*

tively hot month of August, Heer and Mevrouw Bekker woke up one morning to find their daughter gone. To their horror, they discovered that she had eloped with a young officer. The scandal was immense, naturally, but church and parents together saw that the two young lovers were properly punished. Betje was brought home, officially censured by the church council, and forbidden to attend religious services for a full year.

It was hardly an auspicious beginning. Betje's parents must have breathed a sigh of relief when in 1759 their daughter at last found the perfect husband. Adriaan Wolff was the minister of the little town of De Beemster; he was important locally, respectable, prosperous, and surprisingly literate. In fact, it was because they had corresponded on the relation of language to poetry that the couple had met. Of course, there was a little fly in the ointment: the groom was a fifty-two-year-old widower, the bride only twenty-one.

Still, the Wolffs seem to have been happy enough. In 1763 Betje published her first book, a volume of verse entitled *Reflections on Happiness* and subtitled *Letters on the Path to True Happiness*. It is made very clear that Christian morality is the path in question. To modern eyes the heavy, pedantic style and conventional content are unalluring. They struck just the right note in Holland, though, and at once enabled Betje Wolff to join the elite of the literati.

In 1768 Betje started writing under a pseudonym in the magazine *De Gryzaard*. Perhaps the anonymity helped; at any rate, she was using a new style, more realistic, more descriptive, and far more entertaining than her earlier work. Within a year, leaving Christian verse behind, she published under her own name a poem entitled *Walcheren*, after the island in the North Sea, whose beauties she describes at length. It was an immediate success, went into several editions, and made Betje Wolff famous.

Both in her articles and in *Walcheren*, the influence of English literature became evident. More people in Holland spoke English than any other language because of the Netherlands's extensive trade with England. Perhaps that had made it easier for Betje to buy English books. At any rate,

This austere environment should have been the very last to nurture a woman writer. Surely no one thought, when Elisabeth Bekker was born in Vlissingen during the summer of 1738, that the baby would grow up to be more than a housewife. Her parents belonged to the fairly prosperous middle class and gave their daughter the standard minimal education. But the girl seems to have been anxious to learn: at the age of sixteen she could already read English. Then, very properly, she became an active member of the local Dutch Reformed Church. She had reached adulthood.

Just how adult she had in fact become, her parents soon found out. A year later, in the rela-

while everybody else was imitating the French, she remained British in her preferences.

Curiously, after her great success, she again stopped publishing. But in 1776 she started corresponding with another literary woman, Agathe (Aagje) Denken. When Adriaan Wolff finally died, in April, 1777, Aagje promptly moved in with Betje. From then on the two women were as one, sharing not only their lives but their writing.

Still, three years passed before they published anything, and then it was a volume of critical essays, followed soon after by a volume of moral folk songs. Finally, in 1782 they produced their first novel, *The History of Sara Burgerhart.* It was an instant success, ran through several editions, and was even translated into French—the greatest compliment that the French could pay a foreign writer.

This epistolary novel, unlike Betje's earlier work, still reads well today. Its lively and amusing style, its vivid characters, the richness and diversity of its incidents are all clearly influenced by Richardson's novels. It has an attractive freshness, an ability to look at life realistically, that flesh out the moral principles the book is supposed to expound.

Of course, epistolary novels were nothing new; from Laclos to Rousseau, letters had become a common literary form. But the point of view expressed here is in fact new and different. At a time when sentimentality was the fashion, *Sara Burgerhart*'s characters are straightforward, clear-eyed, and on the whole, cheerful. They do not lapse into that cynicism which, in France at least, was prevalent. We are presented with a real world, inhabited by real people who have both good and bad luck, but are made virtuous in the end. As for the heroine, she is neither Rousseau's good savage nor the wicked, sophisticated seductress of Laclos's or Restif's dreams. In fact, she behaves quite normally: she is almost seduced by an attractive young man but resists at the last moment and is rewarded with a happy marriage. Under its eighteenth-century accouterments, this is the first nineteenth-century middle-class novel—a sort of Dickensian world inhabited by Betje Wolff's contemporaries.

As in Dickens, a sharp distinction is drawn between good and evil. There is little room for ambiguity, none for people who are morally indifferent. Each character quickly reveals his raison d'être. Sara speaks for innocence and candor; Blankaart, her tutor, for no-nonsense experience; the anonymous Mr. R. for vice and perversion. Even the names point the moral: Burgerhart means "middle-class heart"—an honest, hard-working, virtuous person devoid of the vices prevalent in the aristocracy. The young man whom Sara marries in the end is named Edeling—"noble." Buigzaam, the name of Sara's woman lodger, means "flexible"; she has allowed her parents to talk her into marriage with a rich but dissolute young man, and consequently she has had a miserable life.

There is another peculiarity which distinguishes *Sara Burgerhart* from other contemporary novels: it is apparently written from a conservative and even anti-feminist viewpoint. "The unprejudiced observer of mankind," it says, "sees only too well that a marked inequality is necessary between men, that there must be differences in rank, and that wealth must be unevenly distributed. He does not yearn for an impossible equality, but he tries to bring happiness to those around him." Rousseau would have been deeply shocked—and incensed.

Worse still is a diatribe against an overeducated woman which, by implication, attacks all feminine learning. "She has much nonfeminine knowledge . . . and receives many letters from learned men. She assumes a sort of authority which we are all too glad to allow her: in one word, Miss Hartog is a learned woman of the most unpleasant kind, who calls all the poets rhyme-makers and good-for-nothings." One can only suppose that the resentment is directed at some long-forgotten critic of Betje Wolff's early verse; unfortunately it reads like an attack on all cultivated women.

More important, although *Sara Burgerhart* embodies the rather stale, conventional spirit of the *Path to True Happiness,* it succeeds as a book because it clothes this spirit in a lively and convincing literary expression. The covers of the eighteenth-century editions bear the words "Niet vertaalt" ("Not translated," meaning that this is an original Dutch work instead of a translation)— an eloquent comment on the current state of the written word in the Netherlands.

It is curious that compared with the author's life, the book's attitude is uncompromisingly moral, even puritanical. Sara triumphs at the end only because she has been tempted but has overcome that temptation; yet Betje surely remembered her own elopement. Then too, it is hard not to wonder just what her relationship was with Aagje Denken. The two women lived together, worked together, never left each other's side. After that brief, possibly unfulfilled youthful episode, Betje's only partner had been an elderly man. She was, after all, only thirty-nine when her husband died and her friend moved in. While nothing is known, it seems not impossible that Aagje and Betje's relationship was one of love as well as friendship. In all probability, they would not even have seen it as a deviation from the virtue they so constantly extolled: only men could sully. Sexually, women may well not have counted.

Be that as it may, the success of *Sara Burgerhart* encouraged the authors; they quickly produced two more novels, one in 1785, the other in 1787. Then Prussian troops moved into the little town in which they had settled after Pastor Wolff's death. In what must have seemed to them a radical step, Betje and Aagje determined to resettle in France. While anybody else would have made straight for Paris, the two ladies decided that the capital was too big, too bad, too glamorous. Instead, they moved to Trévoux, a little town near Lyons that had once been famous for the excellence of its Jesuit school.

France in 1788 might not have seemed the ideal place to take up residence. Even before the Revolution actually started, there had been sporadic outbursts of violence everywhere. However, the countryside was evidently quiet enough for the two women to behave like good tourists and write about what they had seen. In 1789 they produced *Wandelingen door Bourgogne (Wanderings Through Burgundy)*, which was well received in the

Netherlands.

As a tourist guide, however, it came at the wrong moment. By the end of 1789, foreigners who didn't have a good reason to be in France were careful to stay away. Soon people were being arrested in droves. Lyons, having remained firmly royalist in conviction, found itself the target of violent denunciations by the radicals. While the country seethed around them, Aagje and Betje were happily embarked on yet another long and moral tale, *The History of Cornelia Wildschut,* the six volumes of which came out in the Netherlands between 1793 and 1796.

Of course, it was not nearly as dangerous to be a foreigner in France (unless you were English or Austrian) as it was to be French. As an outsider you were considered politically uninvolved and therefore safe from prosecution. It was especially good to be Dutch, since Holland was already a republic. Then in 1794–95, French armies marched through Belgium, invaded Holland, and founded the Batavian Republic. Having made sure that a sizable tribute was paid to the French government, they declared the Netherlands a sister and an ally. Obviously the two authors were safe, but it can hardly have been pleasant, even in Trévoux, when Lyons was virtually razed to the ground by a Jacobin army and renamed Free City as a punishment for its reactionary opinions.

Until now, Betje Wolff had depended financially on income from various family inheritances; her husband had left nothing to speak of. Though she was a best-selling author, her literary income was always tiny. Unlike writers today, eighteenth-century authors received no royalties: they sold their work for a flat fee to a bookseller and publisher, who reaped all future profits. Even a phenomenally successful writer like Voltaire had to find other sources of income in order to live. When books were translated into a foreign language, as *Sara Burgerhart* was into German in 1796, the author received next to nothing. This wouldn't have mattered except that in 1794 the Dutch businessman with whom Betje's funds were invested went bankrupt. By 1797 it was painfully clear that the two women were ruined. Leaving Trévoux, they moved back to The Hague.

Since writing would not support them, Betje valiantly turned to translations. She produced a whole series of them, for Dutch literature was still extremely sparse. Naturally they didn't pay much either, and the two women found it almost impossible to make ends meet. In France, literary figures in similar straits were often assisted by wealthy patrons or even a government pension, but it never occurred to the rich Dutch merchants who still ran the country to come to the help of the best-known living Dutch writer.

Still, Betje managed to do a little writing. Her *Songs and Poems for the Fatherland* came out in 1798. At last, in 1801, she received an inheritance large enough to live on comfortably: it was only just in time. She had begun to suffer from a painful, slow disease, but she went on working. The first two volumes of *The Writings of an Elderly Woman* came out in 1802. Two more were left unfinished, for Betje's sufferings were too great. On November 5, 1804, she died. It was more than Aagje Denken could bear: six days later she joined her friend.

Today Betje Wolff is an obscure name outside Holland, and little known even in her own country. But her work sold throughout the nineteenth century, and a new edition of *Sara Burgerhart* which came out in 1905 did so well that it had to be reprinted the following year. More remarkable than this prolonged popularity is the fact that in an austere, unliterary country, it was a woman who not only produced the best books of her time, but also managed to achieve a new kind of freedom through talent alone. It never occurred to Betje Wolff that she was less gifted than men, or that her sex precluded success, or that women weren't supposed to write books. Just as Mme de Pompadour felt no hesitation in helping to rule France, so Betje Wolff unhesitatingly created her own place in what had, with exceedingly few exceptions, been an all-male profession.

Madame Necker

Switzerland was generally considered a small, uninteresting country full of mountains and Protestants, but in 1780, as any well-informed Parisian would have told you, it had at least three claims to fame. One was an illustrious doctor, Tronchin, who gave up the silly paraphernalia of current medicine and actually started to cure his patients. The second was that most famous of writers, the great Jean Jacques Rousseau. The third, Jacques Necker, was busy saving France at the moment; but as he blandly informed the King, his wife, Suzanne, was doing half the work. The only question, really, is whether she wasn't doing all of it.

Ten years later the same Parisian would still have admired Tronchin and Rousseau, but he would have told you angrily that the fool, the incompetent Necker, had fortunately gone home to Geneva. This decline in Necker's standing was due to the collapse of the first successful publicity campaign of modern times. The product had failed to perform as admirably as the public had been led to expect, and the party responsible for the hoax had been no other than Madame Necker.

Suzanne Necker decided early on that her husband should rule France. In what was to prove a much-used argument, she explained to everyone that since her husband was good at making money as a private banker, he would be equally good at balancing the state budget. Of course, it was not enough for her to expound on her husband's greatness: in those days, since there were no mass media in which to advertise, you needed a successful salon where you could display and promote your product. That is just what Mme Necker created from scratch in 1767, although to do it she had had to come a very long way.

Suzanne Curchod was born in 1732, the daughter of a Swiss Calvinist minister, and was brought up at home by her admirably literate father. By the age of sixteen she could read and write Latin fluently, knew some Greek, was competent in mathematics and the natural sciences,

Duplessis. *M. Necker.*
Photograph courtesy of Musées Nationaux, Paris

Duplessis. *Mme Necker.*
Photograph courtesy of Musées Nationaux, Paris

painted, and played both the violin and the harpsichord. She was remarkably pretty and from her middle teens was surrounded by a steady crowd of suitors with whom she flirted enthusiastically. As soon as they became serious, however, she withdrew, managing to be coy, provocative, and ice-cold all at the same time. Nor was there any chance of her eloping with a handsome young man as Betje Wolff had done: the physical side of love seemed distinctly unappealing to Suzanne.

It was apparently no hardship for Mlle Curchod to remain unmarried. At twenty-five—still single, bright, and pretty—she moved to Lausanne, hardly a great metropolis, but a relatively cheerful and civilized town where people led much freer lives than in neighboring Geneva. There she was an instant hit. She joined the Academy of the Waters, a group of young people whose members, with the exception of Suzanne, often continued their theoretical discussions of love by looking into its more practical applications. Perhaps because of Mlle Curchod's mixture of intelligence, good looks, and virtue, she was soon elected president of the academy and became something of a celebrity.

Just at this time, a rather odd-looking young man—all cheeks and no features—chanced to visit Lausanne. "He has nice hair, a pretty hand, and the appearance of a man of good birth," Mlle Curchod wrote about him. "His expression is so singular and intelligent that I don't know anyone who is like him. . . . The variety of his mental acquirements is prodigious." She was undoubtedly right: Edward Gibbon, the future author of *The Decline and Fall of the Roman Empire,* was indeed a remarkable person. Suzanne, who after all was past the normal age of marriage, saw her chance: he was well bred, his family had money, he would make a perfect husband.

As for young Gibbon, he was instantly smitten. He tells us in his memoirs that "the wit, the beauty, and erudition of Mlle Curchod were the theme of universal applause. The report of such a prodigy awakened my curiosity; I saw and I loved." Soon it was settled. Suzanne was in love, intellectually if not physically, and Gibbon went home to tell his father. Perhaps, after all,

Lecour. *A Walk in the Palais Royal Gardens.* One of the fashionable parks in Paris where people came to see and be seen, it was open until late at night for the opera audiences who liked to stroll there. The Metropolitan Museum of Art, New York. The Elisha Whittelsey Collection, The Elisha Whittelsey Fund, 1964 (64.550.6)

his passion was not devouring. For when the elder Gibbon informed his son that he could never agree to the marriage, the young man "sighed as a lover and . . . obeyed as a son." Luckily, he wrote, "the remedies of absence and time were at length effectual."

This might be all very well for the future historian, but Suzanne was crushed when she received a letter which opened with: "I cannot begin! And yet I must. I take up my pen, I put it down, I take it up again. You perceive at once what I am going to say. Spare me the rest." The letter then went on for several pages to embroider on the same theme. It was at this stage in Suzanne's life that her peculiar personality, a blend of coldness and hysteria, of rationalism and abandoned romanticism, asserted itself. At the moment, its most visible component was a wild and spectacular despair manifested through what contemporaries called nervous prostration—depression so severe as to be akin to a nervous breakdown.

In 1760 Pastor Curchod died, leaving his family destitute. It was unexampled for a girl of good family to go to work in order to support herself, but Mlle Curchod bravely undertook to give lessons to upper-class children. Perhaps because it appealed to that earnest streak in the Swiss character, this move led Lausanne society to regard her with more enthusiasm than ever. Still, it was all pretty hard, and Suzanne took it out on her mother, who died in 1763. The last element of Mlle Curchod's character was now in place: she never stopped feeling guilty, never stopped reproaching herself. Consequently she found herself exceptionally well placed to notice other people's bad behavior.

In May, 1763, Gibbon came back to Geneva, and Suzanne, who had developed a grandiloquent, hysterical writing style, promptly sent him a long letter. "I blush at the step I am taking," she wrote. "I would like to hide it from you, I would like to hide it from myself. Is it possible, great God! that an innocent heart should abase itself to this point? . . . I beg you on my knees to release my crazed heart from its doubts. Sign the complete admission of your indifference and my soul will become reconciled to its fate." Gibbon hadn't heard from her in six years; understandably he recoiled: the letter was never answered.

That silence made it even more awkward when, in August, Gibbon and Mlle Curchod found themselves face to face. For some time now, Suzanne had been teaching the children of Pastor Moulton, a most unusual man who managed to be an intimate friend of Rousseau's while remaining on good terms with Voltaire, whom he visited at Ferney every Saturday. For a while he had been taking the governess along, thus giving her a priceless introduction to the most famous writer in Europe. This time Gibbon made himself plain: he had no intention of ever marrying Mlle Curchod, but he did want to be her friend. Mastering her hysteria, the lady agreed, and Gibbon turned out to be one of the ornaments of her Paris salon.

Now the thirty-two-year-old Mlle Curchod was finding herself in a predicament: she was reaching what was then considered middle age, and she was still unmarried. Giving up on Switzerland, she went to work for a rich young widow, Mme de Vermenoux, who moved to Paris in June, 1764. There the governess felt altogether lost. She hated her job but could not afford to quit. She realized that her clothes were grotesquely old-fashioned but could not afford to replace them. Worse, she had lost the admiring society which had until then made her life bearable. "I came to Paris after having been very popular," she wrote, "but I didn't know a single one of the things that were either useful or necessary to me. . . . I blushed at the smallness of my mind and opinions." Things looked bleak indeed for Mlle Curchod when, fortunately, the dullest man Mme de Vermenoux had ever met came courting that wealthy widow. His name was Jacques Necker, and he was a business associate of one of her cousins.

Except for his money, M. Necker appeared to be no prize. This plump, chinless man who looked a little like a solemn turkey was devoid of conversation, learning, or wit. He dressed badly, lived plainly, didn't even have a mistress, and would have been completely out of place in Paris if the government's financial system had been a little more effective. Luckily for him, it wasn't.

It was widely believed in Catholic countries that lending at interest was a sin, so it was left to the Protestants to run the banks. There M. Necker had a marked advantage, being not only the son of a Swiss law professor but a Calvinist as well. At the age of fifteen he entered the Banque Vernet as a clerk. He was exceptionally hardworking and soon rose to a superior rank; then in 1762–63, he managed to make himself almost 2 million livres.

His method was simplicity itself, and by no means original. By bribing a highly placed official in the foreign ministry, he always knew exactly how close France was to peace with England, and he bought or sold English government bonds accordingly. When the official in question found out the size of M. Necker's profit, he shrieked that he had been robbed of the half share he had been told to expect. Still, it was not considered that the banker had done anything illegal, since everyone knew that officials were corrupt by definition. It was no crime to take advantage of the situation—though it came very close.

In 1762 the proprietor, Vernet, passed the bank on to his nephew Thélusson, and M. Necker bought a quarter share in the business. Then in 1764 the crops failed, with consequent speculation and a swift rise in prices. Jacques Necker knew a good thing when he saw it: by the end of the panic he had tripled his fortune, once again quite legally. That people starved because wheat prices were deliberately inflated was an unfortunate but acceptable side effect; Thélusson was so convinced of it that in 1765 Necker was put in sole charge of the bank. He was now a very rich man.

Still, money wasn't enough; and M. Necker was smart enough to realize that as long as he was by himself, society would remain closed to him. Clearly he needed a wife. On the advice of Thélusson, he decided to try his charms and fortune on Mme de Vermenoux. But since she found him quite deadly, he spent his visits talking to the governess. She was pretty, she was smart, she was reassuringly Swiss: to everyone's surprise, he proposed. Of course Suzanne accepted him, and Mme de Vermenoux could only comment: "They will

Moreau le Jeune. *An Elegant Supper.* The crowning glory of a fashionable day, the supper was eaten around nine or ten o'clock in an atmosphere of relaxed conviviality. It could be the prelude to more amorous exercises.
The Metropolitan Museum of Art, New York. Purchase, 1934 (34.22.2)

bore each other to death; at least it will give them something to do."

Seldom has anyone been so wrong. In its own peculiar way, the Neckers' marriage proved to be a—well-advertised—model of connubial bliss. Suzanne was far and away Jacques's intellec-tual superior, but she respected his ability to make money. Besides, she saw that while each of them would fail alone, together they could con-quer Paris. This is what she set out to do.

As for M. Necker, he must sometimes have found Suzanne a little trying. The evening before

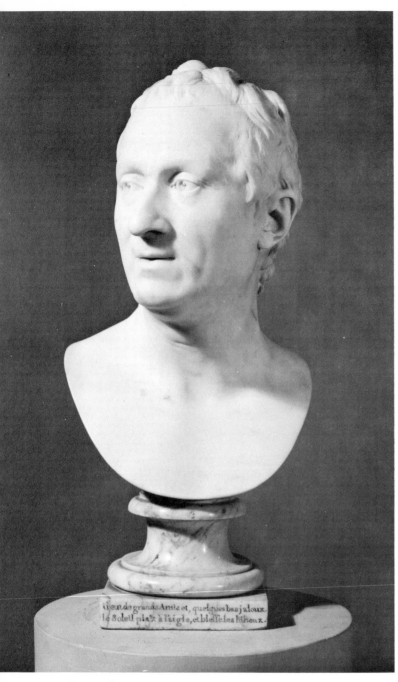

Houdon. *Diderot.*
The Metropolitan Museum of Art, New York.
Gift of Mr. and Mrs. Charles Wrightsman, 1974 (1974.291)

their wedding, she sent him this letter: "O my Jacques! Allow me to enjoy my happiness without thinking about it. The day when you cease to love me, if it comes, would make Nature itself foreign to me. When I wake up, my first thought is toward heaven, my soul blends with the earth and draws a new fervor from this union. Let the moment of my death become the highest degree of your love and it will be the finest day of my life." It is hardly usual for prospective brides to look forward to their demise—a moment which henceforth seemed to fascinate Suzanne. Had he been less self-satisfied, M. Necker might have found the communication singularly daunting. The wedding took place as planned, however, and within days the new Mme Necker penned a description of her husband in what one can only suppose to have been a spirit of fun and irony. The trouble with this remarkably sharp little text is that, far from being an exaggeration, it is altogether accurate. People who both knew and disliked M. Necker in the seventies or eighties would have quite agreed with it. Mme Necker wrote:

> Picture to yourself the most humorless fellow in the whole world, so completely persuaded of his own superiority that he does not even see mine [that, if true, was swiftly rectified]; so convinced of his own powers of penetration that he is forever being fooled; so certain that he possesses every talent in the highest degree of perfection that he does not look elsewhere for instruction; never astonished at the littleness of others because he is always enveloped in his own greatness; ever comparing himself to those about him so that he may have the pleasure of seeing that no comparison is possible; confounding men of parts with the ignorant because he thinks himself to be placed upon a mountain, and that all creatures inferior to himself must not be on the same level with him; preferring fools also because they make a more striking contrast with his own genius; and with all this as capricious as a pretty woman.

For a wife with Mme Necker's ambition, such a man might have seemed like unpromising material, but M. Necker had a crucial redeeming quality: in a world where everyone talked, and talked well, he remained silent. In no time people began to think what Mme Necker tirelessly hinted to them: that M. Necker was concerned with matters so deep that he couldn't bother coming down to the level of ordinary conversation. The less M. Necker said, the faster his reputation as a genius grew. Mme Necker had thus invented the two guiding principles of modern advertising: she fooled the public about the actual usefulness of her product, and by making it seem indispensable, she created a demand where none had existed.

Of course, unlike modern advertising agencies, Mme Necker had to rely on word of mouth. But after all, the people whose opinion counted all lived in Paris and Versailles. If they could be persuaded to attend the Neckers' salon, then little by little the word would spread, and within a few years, the successful if slightly crooked banker would become a selfless genius—the only man capable of running the country. That M. Necker shared his wife's ambitions is beyond question. He thought the world of himself, but without her diverse skills, he would have remained a millionaire banker.

At first nothing much happened: Suzanne was finding her footing, asserting control over M. Necker, and then, in the fall, fighting the disgust caused by her pregnancy. Her daughter Germaine, the future Mme de Staël, was born in April, 1766. Since Mme Necker had naturally read the newly published *Emile,* Jean Jacques Rousseau's book on the education of children, she decided to breastfeed the baby. After three months, however, it was noticed that the baby was starving. Hiring a stout, healthy nurse, Mme Necker was able to return to her main object.

First, in 1767 the Neckers went on a trip to Switzerland. When they came back, the banker had been appointed minister of the republic of Geneva to the court of Versailles. This not only gave him entree into government circles, but also instantly made him a diplomat, and thus, in a status-conscious society, much more respectable than a mere businessman. The next year the Neckers moved from the unfashionable Marais to a sumptuous townhouse in the chic rue de Cléry: the proper setting for the salon had been established. Finally, in 1769 M. Necker was appointed director of the French East India Company, a post that carried great prestige.

All this time, Mme Necker was working hard on her salon. She was pretty and flirtatious (but virtuous); she could spend a great deal of money; and she was intelligent. Now she had to find the right sort of guests. They could not be great aristocrats, who would have looked down on the middle-class Neckers. It was the intellectuals who were glad to come, talk, and spread rumors about this new star on the social horizon. By 1770 Mme Necker had selected Friday as the day when her house was always open. Through this choice she avoided competing with the other salons, and, being a Protestant, she was able to serve meat (a great attraction) on a day when Catholics were supposed to eat fish. Soon she was receiving d'Alembert, Diderot, Buffon (the great naturalist), Marmontel, Grimm (whose letters spread the salon's fame all over Europe), and, when he was in Paris, her old friend Gibbon.

One name was missing. Voltaire might be living in Ferney, but no one could boast of being really *à la page* who did not at least correspond with him. In April, 1770, Mme Necker gave a dinner at which it was decided to commission a statue of the great man. Voltaire was delighted and obligingly wrote Suzanne; the trick was done.

Acquiring intellectuals was only her first step. They created the right atmosphere and spread praise of M. Necker, but even better, they were themselves an attraction to the people who really mattered. By 1773 Mme de Vermenoux commented, "[Mme Necker's] fame grows day by day. Her taste for writers and philosophers is unchanged, but she has now acquired a fondness for society women who are reputed to be witty." In this age when women exerted an often decisive influence, nothing could have been smarter. By the time Louis XV died in 1774, Mme Necker had one of the most fashionable salons in Paris; even Mme du Deffand was content to be seen there—a mark that the Neckers had arrived. And unlike the marquise, Mme Necker had had neither aristocratic connections nor royal lovers.

What was her salon actually like? One of its habitués, the abbé Galiani, gives us a picture in

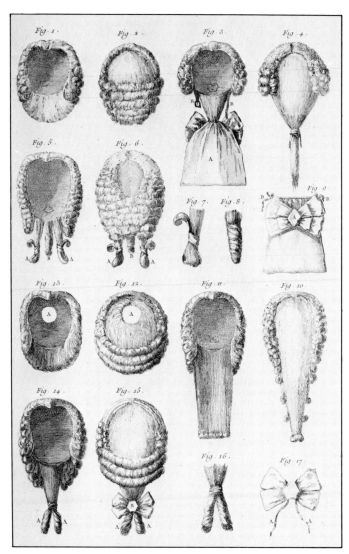

Wigs, a plate from the *Encyclopédie* illustrating the varieties of men's wigs that were fashionable in the 1750s. Thomas J. Watson Library, The Metropolitan Museum of Art, New York

a letter he wrote Mme Necker from Naples, where he had reluctantly returned:

A Friday does not pass but I go to you in spirit. I arrive and find you, one minute, adjusting your dress; the next minute you are lying on the *duchesse* [a kind of chaise longue]. I seat myself at your feet. Thomas [a fashionable poet] groans to himself silently; Morellet storms with passion. Grimm and Suard laugh heartily and my friend Creutz [the Swedish ambassador] notices nothing. . . . Dinner is announced. We go in. The others eat meat, I abstain; but while I am admiring the ardor with

which the abbé Morellet cuts up the turkey, I eat so much of that Scotch green codfish . . . that I get an attack of indigestion. We rise from the table and drink our coffee, everyone speaking at the same time. The abbé Raynal agrees with me that Boston and English America are forever separated from England; and at the same time Creutz and Marmontel agree that Grétry is the Pergolese of France. M. Necker thinks it is all very well; he nods and goes away.

That, of course, was the trick: by remaining silent, often while sucking on his thumb, M. Necker avoided saying something stupid. Mme Necker made sure everyone knew that M. Necker was a genius by referring to his deep studies, wise reflections, and ceaseless efforts. Another woman might not have been believed, but Mme Necker was so fierce, so insistent that it was safer to take her word if you wanted to go on frequenting her salon. Besides, in an age when husbands and wives were automatically unfaithful, the Neckers' extraordinary and unbroken conjugal bliss was an object of increasing wonder. Suzanne, after all, was very attractive: if M. Necker could command so perfect a loyalty, then he must be a most unusual man.

What no one saw was that the Neckers' life wasn't always enjoyable: Mme Necker's morbid preoccupation with death and her frequent bouts of depression combined to make her husband suffer. Moreover, her afflictions grew steadily worse because Suzanne now had the most galling of rivals, her own daughter Germaine.

There was no question of hiring a governess to raise the little girl. Mme Necker's sense of duty was too strong for that, and it might also have been a constant reminder of her own unfortunate years as a governess. But the consequence was that the child, who attended the salon after studying all day, became an alien presence intruding between husband and wife. Nor did it help when it became obvious not only that Germaine was unusually bright, but also that she much preferred her father. Who wouldn't have? Here is Germaine's later description of her mother, thinly disguised as Lady Edgerton in *Corinne:* "She never tired of taking all joy out of life by making the

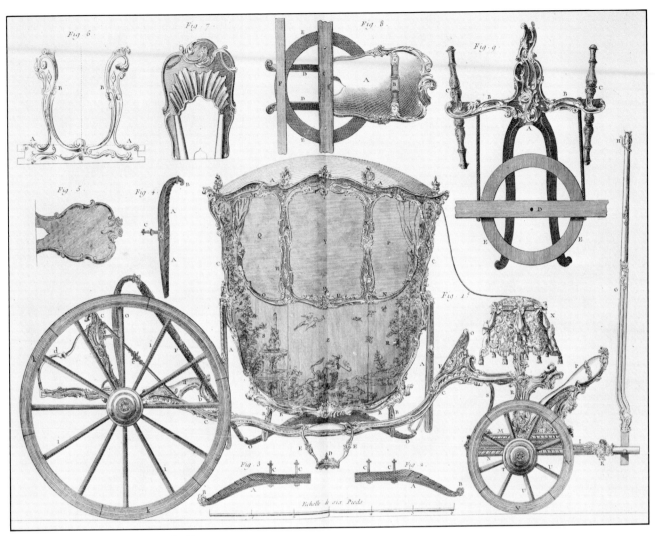

Carriage, a plate from the *Encyclopédie.*
This gala town berline was used on grand occasions.
Thomas J. Watson Library,
The Metropolitan Museum of Art, New York

least pleasure a subject of reproach and by pre-
scribing some duty to make up for every hour
employed in any activity that differed from the
day's routine." The key word is "duty." Like
many people who crucify their families on this
dubious altar, Mme Necker made very sure that
love was linked to sacrifice and suffering. She herself had her periodic collapses which could be as-
cribed to the wickedness of her entourage. As for
what she felt, she made it clear in this characteristic outburst: "Oh, my God, end without pain a
life which you have filled with your favors but

which is poisoned by remorse, memories, the contempt and ingratitude of others."

No such conflicts, however, were allowed to
show beyond the family circle. To everyone else,
Mme Necker was the ecstatically happy spouse of
a great genius. She made it so obvious that Marmontel, for instance, could write: "It was not for
us, and not for herself that Mme Necker worked
so hard, it was for her husband." In the seventies,
all those efforts paid off. In 1772 M. Necker sold
his share of the Banque Thélusson and announced
that henceforth he would have nothing more to

Lavréince. *The Musicale*. Among a number of social innovations introduced in the second half of the eighteenth century was the invitation to a private concert. The Metropolitan Museum of Art, New York. Harris Brisbane Dick Fund, 1935 (35.100.16)

do with moneymaking. In fact, he was leaving the management of his entire fortune to that wise and wonderful woman, his wife. Now it should be clear to everyone that he was available to take on the government of France.

In spite of the most active propaganda, however, he had to wait another five years. When Louis XVI succeeded to the throne, he entrusted the ministry of finance to a well-known reformer, M. Turgot, who, with the support of the *Encyclopédistes,* tried to reform the state. The Queen and the court, who liked things the way they were, saw to it that he was fired. The treasury, as usual, was broke, and M. Necker had his chance. Since he was a Protestant, he could not under French law become a member of the King's council. So Louis XVI gave him a new title, general director of finance, and saw him privately instead of in session with the other ministers. The Neckers moved into the Hôtel du Contrôle Général (a hôtel was a large private house) and proceeded to revel in their power, fame, and achievements.

First they bought the château of Saint-Ouen, which had belonged to Mme de Pompadour. Then they proceeded to make it known that the wise and selfless M. Necker, who had refused to take the large salary attached to his office, was saving the catastrophically disorganized national finances and that for a good deal of his work he relied on Mme Necker.

Before looking at his performance, it should be said that M. Necker had good intentions and even an occasional good idea. In a country utterly without representative institutions, for instance, he wanted to set up local elected bodies as the first step to an English-style parliament. But the French Parlement, a nonelected body of rich and selfish men who had bought their offices, soon put a stop to this, and the King was too weak to fight them.

When it comes to finance, however, M. Necker's incompetence is all too clear. First he announced that he was stopping the dreadful waste of money that was going on at Versailles and hinted that he often refused to give money to Marie Antoinette herself. Since the Queen was well known as a spendthrift, this made him immediately popular; the only trouble is that he was lying.

It is true that the new director of finance tried to reduce some minor expenditures. When the Queen wanted the King to give a large dowry to one of her protégées, for example, he persuaded Louis XVI to make the groom a duke instead. But since M. Necker was shrewd enough to remember Turgot's end, he always made it a point to give Marie Antoinette more money than she actually requested.

In order to establish the state's credit, M. Necker spent more lavishly than ever so that people would take it as a sign that the financial crisis was over. It wasn't: the deficit, swelled by huge expenditures on the American war, was financed by borrowing at ever higher rates of interest, thereby increasing the yearly outlays and building up a mountain of mostly short-term debt. It was the best possible recipe for a crash; but for a time the public, which had been accustomed to chronic, well-advertised shortages at the treasury, thought M. Necker a magician. In fact, what he had done was to set up the great financial crisis of the late eighties, which in turn brought on the Revolution.

M. Necker's popularity, already high, was inflated to idolatry in 1781 when he published his *Compte-rendu au Roi.* For the first time in the history of the French monarchy, the budget was made visible to all. Or so it seemed. In fact, M. Necker had carefully rearranged the figures. By overstating and anticipating income, fudging expenditures, and hiding the amount of the national debt, he made it look as if he had balanced the budget. People believed him and praised him to the skies. Unfortunately for him, the only person who really mattered was furious; Louis XVI had not expected the outcry which followed the revelation that huge sums were spent on the numerous royal households and the pensions of the aristocracy. When the protests came, he didn't hesitate; he simply fired M. Necker.

The Neckers were outraged, but they knew it was simply a question of time before the great man was called back to deal with the mess he had left behind. In the meantime, both Mme Necker and their daughter Germaine spread the word that the genius who alone had put national finances on a sound basis was now needed more than ever, since his successors were making the most ghastly mistakes. Louis XVI didn't agree, however, and he made up in obstinacy for the intelligence he lacked.

During the years away from office, Mme Necker had other occupations. The triumph of her salon, while it was no doubt gratifying, had never caused her to forget what she really was: a Swiss Calvinist. It had not helped her transcend what she could never overcome: the guilt caused by the way she had treated her mother. Besides, although she liked being rich, she had a social conscience. Inaugurating a practice which later flourished in the United States, she decided to improve the lot of the poor. In 1778 she opened the first true hospital that Paris had ever seen.

In the eighteenth century the rich who became sick were cared for at home by their own doctors. The poor of Paris were sent to the church-run Hôtel-Dieu, a place so sordid, so filthy, and so brutal that even the homeless poor went there only to die. Mme Necker, who appears to have had genuine charitable impulses, decided that something more was needed. First she had to negotiate with the archbishop of Paris, since nuns were the only nurses allowed by custom. She accomplished this successfully, no mean trick for a Calvinist. Then, having produced a large sum of money, she did all the work and gave her husband all the credit.

"Our Hôtel-Dieu in Paris," she wrote, "is a place of misery; there are up to eight patients to a bed. M. Necker is trying to reform this disorder; but to do so, it must be proved that the poor can be treated one to a bed. This can only be proved by actually doing it. I have taken this upon myself." Later she added: "[We have] airy rooms, without noises or smells. The sick are treated with the greatest cleanliness and with all the care necessary to their being cured. . . . [They are] fed healthy meals and given the best possible medicines."

Mme Necker deserves a great deal of credit, both for alleviating dreadful suffering and for establishing the first decent, clean, and humane hospital in France. From 1778, when she first opened the Hospice de la Charité, to 1788, when her health forced her to leave it, she assiduously supervised her hospital, with its 8 large rooms and 128 beds. After the Revolution, when Mme Necker had long been dead, the hospice was re-titled, very appropriately, the Hôpital Necker, a name that it bears today.

In the late eighties, luckily for the Neckers, the treasury encountered growing difficulties. In 1788 Louis XVI called the first meeting of the Estates-General in almost two hundred years, and since the problem was entirely financial, he also recalled M. Necker. The minister's reappearance was greeted with ecstasy by almost everyone: he was incorruptible, he understood money, he wanted to reform all the current abuses. Mme Necker changed the nature of her salon so that it became exclusively political and represented advanced liberal ideas. All the young aristocrats who had fought with or supported the American insurgents congregated there. The necessary reforms were discussed feverishly, a new climate of opinion was created. M. Necker found all the support he needed. And when the King tried to fire him in 1789, the outcry was so unanimous, so violent that the poor monarch found himself forced to take the dismissed minister back. Mme Necker had done a good job.

The only thing was, public opinion had become a lot harder to manipulate now that the National Assembly looked at the state's accounts. Soon, in a swift and complete reversal, the savior of 1789 became the knave of 1790. M. Necker's profound incompetence, so long and so thoroughly hidden by his ambitious wife, finally came to light.

Everyone had been anxiously awaiting his address on finance at the opening meeting of the Estates-General. Unfortunately, when M. Necker gave up his pregnant silences he turned out to be prolix, obscure, and dull. That might not have mattered much if his actual performance in office had not been so abysmal. This time there could be no question of hidden borrowing, and the miracles of 1777 to 1781 quite failed to recur. Mme Necker still had her salon, of course, but France was no longer governed by the people who came to her dinners, and her propaganda mattered little to the man in the street.

By August, 1790, M. Necker had become so unpopular that Suzanne and he fled, with a good deal of difficulty, and with one arrest on the way, back to Switzerland. There at their château of Coppet they watched the Revolution with increasing horror: it was one thing to be the prime minister of a constitutional monarchy, quite another to see all one's friends going to the guillotine. There were no salons now, no ambitions.

Astonishingly, the Neckers' failure did not change them. Suzanne still ruled Jacques, and both went on behaving as if this were another temporary eclipse, like the one between 1781 and 1788, at the end of which the world would again recognize the great man's genius. As for the new order emerging from the convulsions in France, they failed to understand it—or at least M. Necker did. Suzanne slowly came to realize that nothing could be salvaged from her life's work. She had her husband to herself for a time, since Germaine, now a highly successful hostess, had remained in Paris, but nothing could make up for the collapse of her world.

Soon her nervous disorders worsened. Early in 1794, sure that she was dying, she commanded her husband to have a special building erected to hold two huge stone vats filled with alcohol. Fearful of being buried, Mme Necker asked to be embalmed after death and placed in one of the vats. There, preserved by the alcohol, she could still receive daily visits from her husband. Her wishes were carried out. After she died in May, and until his own death in 1804, M. Necker continued to attend her. When his turn came, he was placed in the second vat. In death as in life, the Neckers' extraordinary partnership endured.

The Flesh Triumphant
Mademoiselle Clairon
Madame du Barry

No one could have been more respectable than Suzanne Necker or Betje Wolff; in that regard, at least, each seems somewhat out of place in the eighteenth century. Mademoiselle Clairon, on the other hand, was thoroughly disreputable and made a career of it, even after she had become a great actress.

If she had not needed money so constantly, surely Mlle Clairon would still have had many lovers. Her ardors were famous. According to a police report dated September 18, 1748: "This woman is well known to have a strong and passionate temperament and to be lascivious in the extreme. She shouts so loudly when she makes love that the neighbors have to close their windows." Perhaps it was just as well; even leading actresses earned only a meager living. If they were young and pretty, it was usual for them to be kept by a rich lover. In Mlle Clairon's case, necessity and pleasure were joined.

Claire Joseph Lerys, who changed her name to Clairon when she went on the stage, was the illegitimate daughter of a seamstress and a sergeant in the French army. She was born in northern France, and when she was twelve she and her mother moved to Paris. There the young girl, looking out at the house across the street, saw an actress rehearsing a part. Struck dumb, she listened to every word, watched every gesture, and when the performance was over, she took to her bed with a high fever. The next morning she told her mother that she would never sew another stitch; from now on, the theater would be her life.

Mme Lerys was horrified, and with reason, for in those days no actress could succeed without a well-placed protector who saw to it that she was given work. All too often, the powerful man tired quickly of his protégée, so that it took rare talent to keep a career going. No actress was paid enough to meet her expenses, since players had to buy their own splendid and costly stage wardrobes. So a rich lover was a necessity—and most

Greuze. *Mlle Clairon.*
Ex coll.: Cailleux, Paris

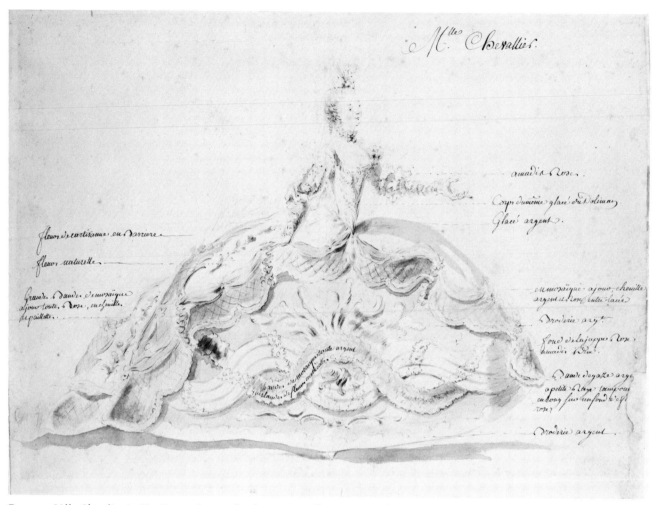

Boquet. *Mlle Chevalier in Her Dance Costume for the King's Ballet.* A good example of eighteenth-century theatrical costume, this ornate and unwieldy dress was actually worn by a ballet dancer. The Metropolitan Museum of Art, New York. Purchase, Mr. and Mrs. Charles Wrightsman Gift, 1966 (66.91)

old actresses were dreadfully poor. Finally, there was that unpleasant consequence, excommunication. For reasons best known to itself, the Catholic church had decided some two hundred years earlier that all actors were automatically excommunicated. They couldn't marry or bear legitimate children since the church controlled all civil ceremonies. For those who cared, excommunication also meant eternal damnation because an actor could neither receive the last rites nor be buried in consecrated ground. A few intellectuals and enlightened *grands seigneurs* may have thought of church services as silly mummeries, but among the people the faith was still profoundly alive.

Although Mme Lerys quailed at the prospects opening before her daughter, there was no stopping the determined girl. On January 8, 1736, at the Comédie Italienne, the thirteen-year-old Clairon gave her first performance, which was a total flop. Realizing that Paris was too hard a nut to crack, she managed to get a job with a troupe of comedians on their way to Rouen. Her mother followed her and there, having given up sewing, they settled down to earn a living.

Clairon was assigned small parts and paid next to nothing, so Mme Lerys, who was a practical woman, opened a lodging house with rooms that anxious people could rent by the hour. It must have been clean and discreet, since it soon became one of the most successful *maisons de passe* in Rouen. Both mother and daughter realized, however, that there were even better ways to make money: a forward-looking fifteen-year-old was an easily marketable commodity.

Naturally, Mlle Clairon presents herself in her memoirs as wholly virtuous. Although her mother tried to sell her virginity, she says, in fact it was love that won the day. But the memoirs are self-serving and, when it comes to Clairon's love life, altogether unconvincing. Virtue and love notwithstanding, the young actress was soon being kept by a succession of men in their fifties while sleeping with anyone else who caught her fancy. "One is alarmed at first," a police agent wrote during one of the troupe's engagements in Lille, "when one sees the rival warriors disputing this woman's heart; but never fear, all will be quietly resolved. The Clairon knows how to arrange these matters and is quite clever enough to manage half a dozen men. And so everything happens in an orderly way to everyone's greatest pleasure."

All this time, Mlle Clairon's other great talent had remained hidden. She was known as a third-rate provincial actress whose stage career was a mere cover for her real activity: prostitution. She was, however, so successful with men that she aroused envy; and from The Hague, where there was no censorship, a brochure appeared entitled *History of Mlle Cronel* [an anagram of the misspelled Clairon], *called Frétillon* [wriggler], *written by herself.* It was an immediate hit.

Obscene pamphlets or songs, printed abroad and smuggled in, were the only way in which disgruntled people could take vengeance on those they resented. Otherwise, the official censors suppressed even mild criticism of anyone with a powerful protector. Far more eminent people than Mlle Clairon—the list might start with Louis XVI and Marie Antoinette—suffered from this form of attack. In the case of poor Clairon, the brochure was remarkably successful, so much so that for the next twenty years *The Life of Frétillon* was periodically updated and republished to take advantage of the heroine's latest adventures, and no wonder. Its descriptions of Frétillon's abundant and varied sex life are both graphic and plausible. As for Clairon, it made her quite frantic.

Aside from amusing everyone in Rouen, *Frétillon* ruined its model's life there. She moved on to Gand where, she claims, her patriotism was offended by the local Anglophilia. It is more likely that she found neither a part nor a rich lover. She had tried the provinces; now only Paris was left. There, at long last, she found her way. A rich *fermier-général,* M. de la Popelinière, whose wife was the duc de Richelieu's mistress, decided to keep her. Soon he introduced her into that peculiar Paris society which consisted of rich men, great nobles, and easy women.

The pretty Mlle Clairon, as everyone discovered, was sexy and amusing. She liked to make love, but she also liked to talk: she was a wonderful companion for a *souper galant* or an evening at the Opéra. In no time M. de la Popelinière, who evidently had no luck with women, lost her to a group of subscribers. Mlle Clairon was extremely expensive, so the prince de Soubise, the duc de Luxembourg, the marquis de Bissy, and the duc de Montmorency-Boutteville, whose families were among the most noble in France, joined together and took shares in her. While the actress was good at attracting men, however, she was terrible at keeping them. Soon the noblemen gave way to more *fermiers-généraux,* who in turn were replaced by successors until it became well established that Clairon had been had by every man in Paris who could pay, along with some who couldn't. Still, it didn't matter. She had made powerful friends, and they eventually introduced her to the duc de Gesvres, the First Gentleman of the Bedchamber, who was in charge of all the theaters in Paris and Versailles. (There were four First Gentlemen, each of whom held office every fourth year. It was during his term of duty that the duc de Richelieu had tried to stop Mme de Pompadour's theatricals.)

The duc de Gesvres, as it happens, was impotent; but apparently Clairon came sufficiently well recommended to succeed anyway. In September, 1743, she was given the *lettre de début* ordering the Comédie Française to take her in.

It was customary for a new actress to choose the role and the play she wanted for her debut, and usually she took an easy secondary part. Mlle Clairon, however, selected the title role in *Phèdre,*

Cochin. *La Princesse de Navarre.* An opera sung, among others,
by Mme de Pompadour. The Metropolitan Museum of Art,
New York. The Elisha Whittelsey Collection,
The Elisha Whittelsey Fund, 1960 (60.622.1)

a part of extreme difficulty normally attempted only by great actresses at the height of their powers. The other actors were horrified, but in spite of their entreaties, she persisted. Since in Paris everyone knew everything, the audience was aware that the little beginner needed a good lesson. As it watched one of the best performances of *Phèdre* ever given, however, the whistles changed to cheers. By the end of her first night on the stage of the Comédie Française, Mlle Clairon had become a star.

No one has ever understood how she did it. Certainly she had worked as an actress all those years in Rouen and Lille, but only in minor parts. Because the great players stayed in Paris, she cannot even have seen much good theater. Nor could she have perfected her technique as a tragic actress in a troupe that played mostly comedies. Now when she tried to play comic roles, she failed miserably; but from the night of her debut, everyone recognized that she and the much older Mlle Dufresnois were the best tragic actresses in Paris.

Needless to say, Clairon promptly realized that she loathed Mlle Dufresnois. In fact she disliked most actors—and always, of course, invented some plausible reason. Through a complicated intrigue, she managed to ruin Granval, a handsome and popular player. Again, she delayed Le Kain's career by some seven years on the grounds that he was too ugly to play tragic roles. There can be no doubt that she was simply jealous: she felt that the public should notice only one person on the stage, and that person was Mlle Clairon.

Still, despite her antics, she soon became enormously popular. A letter, actually the work of a critic but supposedly written to Clairon from the other world by the deceased Mlle Duclos, who had been the leading tragic actress of the twenties and thirties, said: "The tone of your voice, your movements, your eyes, your silences, even, carry the feelings you express into the depths of our souls. Everything tender and pathetic, great and sublime, tragic and terrible is so natural to you that you seem to have been created just to represent it. There is no role you fail to fill . . . with a nobility, a dignity, an intelligence which are

Saint Aubin. *Le Kain.* The Metropolitan Museum of Art, New York. Harris Brisbane Dick Fund, 1917 (17.3.756–1353)

exclusively yours. You are the idol of the public."

It was an enormous achievement. People in the eighteenth century had developed a passion for the theater—private, like Mme de Pompadour's, as well as public. A successful play brought its author instant fame, so that in his lifetime, Voltaire was better known for his third-rate plays than for the work that has made him immortal.

The Paris public, a group of thoroughly experienced theatergoers, was competent, discerning, and tough. The audiences, composed of a mixture of the court and the town, included both intellectuals and ordinary people. Cabals were frequent, jealousies rife. On the other hand, talent was quickly recognized, given great acclaim, and long remembered. The acting techniques of current players were measured against earlier achievements and endlessly discussed. It was possible to become famous overnight, and the atmosphere of the Comédie Française, with its ambitious, bickering, publicity-mad actors, was not unlike that of Hollywood in the twenties and thirties. It differed significantly, however, in that there was no real money to be made.

Comedies were naturally popular, but tragedies were the yardstick by which authors and actors alike were judged. Acting techniques, developed over a century, had become artificial and stereotyped. Instead of speaking their lines naturally, the players were expected to declaim the obligatory alexandrine verse in a monotonous singsong, interrupted by conventional gestures and occasional arbitrary shrieks. Then too, since the plays often portrayed kings and queens, actors were supposed to behave as if they were at Versailles: not a lock of powdered hair must ever be out of place. The result was stilted and unconvincing, as a few avant-garde critics were beginning to realize. Still, Mlle Clairon did what was expected of her, and everyone applauded.

With success, Clairon's circle widened. She still knew (and was kept by) the rich, not always young, men she had met before. But she added a succession of foreigners—Spaniards, Poles, Italians—and all paid through the nose. "All the *agréables,* or those who copy them, want to have Mlle Clairon because it's the smart thing to do; the actress takes them all, because she needs money, she likes them, or needs to satisfy her temperament," the *Observateur des Spectacles* commented. Of course it all made the *Life of Frétillon* even more popular. Anyone who wanted to make fun of Clairon or annoy her could call her Frétillon, and she minded dreadfully.

Still, she enjoyed her new friends and her position as one of the most fashionable women in Paris. The money was nice, too. She moved to a larger apartment and decorated it luxuriously. Of course, every Chinese vase mounted in ormolu, every lacquer table, every pair of silver candlesticks meant a night spent with someone who was willing to pay. A true woman of her century, Clairon took her sex naturally (if more abundantly than most) and cared a great deal about her decor. Owning a dressing table from a good *ébéniste* was important to her, as well as having costly lace for its skirts and silver or gold boxes for her rouge

and powders. She valued luxury far more than stability—and in fact, twice she ran out of money and had to sell everything. She surrounded herself with beautiful things at a time when, more than ever before or since, even the simplest object was a masterpiece of design. Then, of course, there was her wardrobe. Real silk, real brocade, real velvet, real lace—all have practically disappeared from our lives. In the eighteenth century you could buy the most luxurious fabrics and have them embroidered not just with silk, but with gold and silver thread.

Some people, seeing all this luxury, and envious, perhaps, of Clairon's success on the stage, referred to her as a common prostitute. When Marmontel became her lover (not for money; he was brilliant but penniless), one of his friends wrote: "He's become completely unrecognizable ever since he's devoted himself to this whore's amusements." Yet Marmontel, along with many other bright people in Paris, had found that the great actress had a lively and amusing mind. Soon Mlle Clairon's house was frequented not only by the rich and titled, but by the intellectuals as well. Her reputation was securely established when the arbiter of taste and intelligence, Voltaire himself, joined her circle of admirers.

It was no mean achievement. After all, until then actresses had been kept firmly in their place, on the stage or in bed. Now the foreigners who crowded into Paris went to see her perform, called on her at her house, and traveled home with glowing reports. Even at Versailles, where fame was considered rather vulgar, Clairon played again and again before the King.

Succeed she might; but Clairon could never give up the rough-and-tumble side of her life. She had no sooner settled down with the rich M. de Cindré, for instance, than he caught her in bed with the young M. de Jaucourt and threw her out. Suddenly she found herself penniless and had to sell her belongings. It was all right, though; she soon found another wealthy lover. Then there was the Princess Galitzin, a rich Russian lesbian with whom Clairon had a passionate, and well-rewarded, affair.

Still, in spite of her complicated sex life, Clai-

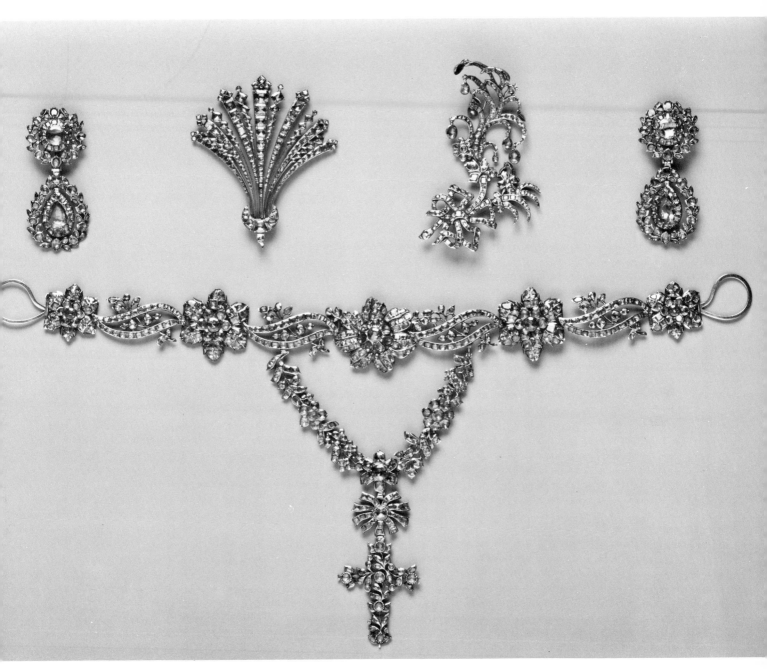

Eighteenth-century gold and garnet necklace, earrings, hair ornament, and aigrette. Private collection, New York

Eisen. *Theatrical Declamation.* It was this sort of artificial exaggeration that Mlle Clairon abandoned for the first time in Bordeaux. The Metropolitan Museum of Art, New York. Harris Brisbane Dick Fund, 1953 (53.600.3302)

ron was the hardest-working actress of her time. Every year she would take the leading role in several new plays, and she was always admirably prepared. It wasn't just that she learned her lines: she studied the characters, lived with them day and night; friends said that she asked for her nightcap in the tones of an empress calling for a cup of poison.

Then around 1750, Clairon took a step that changed the course of French theater. Marmontel loathed the exaggerated singsong traditionally used for reciting tragic verse. Feelings, he kept saying, should seem real, natural. Verse should be spoken with regard for meter but also for verisimilitude. It can all be found in his article on declamation in the *Encyclopédie.* And Clairon listened.

At first she made only small changes in her way of playing. Then in 1752, she was booked to play Agrippina, Nero's mother, in Bordeaux. The first night she played it in the conventional style and was much applauded. The second night, safely away from the sharp eyes of Parisian critics, she tried a revolutionary new method. The singsong was gone, as were the great shrieks of passion: instead, she played a real woman, with real feelings and real reactions. At first, she tells us in her memoirs, the audience watched in surprised silence. Then, slowly, the applause began. At the end of the play it had become a standing ovation.

Still, Bordeaux was one thing and Paris quite another. Bravely she tried her new style onstage at the Comédie Française in Voltaire's latest play, *Electre.* Once again she triumphed, an outcome all the more unlikely because she had not only changed the old way of acting but had also given up the current fashion in theater costumes. Whatever part they played, actors and actresses were used to dressing in corsets, hooped skirts (the men wore short ones), and curled and powdered hair. There was no attempt at local color or historical fidelity. Now after much research, Mlle Clairon dressed like a Greek slave.

"A courageous actress has just done away with the hoop skirt and no one has complained," Diderot wrote. "Ah! If only she dared to show herself . . . in the disorder consequent on so terrible an event as the loss of a son . . . what then would they become, around that wild-looking woman, all those curled and pomaded dolls! Clairon . . . follow your own taste . . . show us nature and truth."

The author was thrilled, and from then on Clairon was his favorite actress. The fact that she was so popular had something to do with it; but also, Voltaire really loved the theater, and he knew that Clairon had improved it beyond recognition. Soon any play in which she took a part was an automatic success. When he saw *L'Orphelin de la Chine,* Collé, a leading critic, wrote: "This tragedy is not good . . . but the actress is admirable. . . . We may even expect perfection from her." After the first night of *Tancrède* (September, 1760), Voltaire must have fainted with joy when he received his mail. "Mlle Clairon was incomparable, even better than she has always been," d'Alembert wrote him, and Diderot: "If you could only see Clairon crossing

the stage, half supported by the executioners around her, her knees giving way under her, her eyes closed, her arms fallen, as if she were dying, if only you could hear her cry when she sees Tancrède."

Now Clairon represented the theater in France. When Mme de Pompadour decided to have a play performed at Choisy, it was Mlle Clairon for whom she sent. When the other actors of the Comédie Française needed something, it was she who was dispatched to Versailles. When an author wanted his play to succeed, he begged her to take a part in it. Even better, money and social acceptance were hers. The duchesse de Gramont, Choiseul's sister, was mad about her; so was that social arbiter, the maréchale de Luxembourg. For the first time ever, an actress born in the gutter, and notorious because of her extraordinary sex life, had moved to the top of the most difficult and

Martin. *Indienne, Zéphyre. Left,* a French idea of the appropriate costume for an Indian woman; *right,* a personification of the warm summer breeze. Both are examples of the kind of theater costumes Diderot disliked so much. The Metropolitan Museum of Art, New York. The Elisha Whittelsey Collection, The Elisha Whittelsey Fund, 1966 (66.614.2)

Moreau le Jeune. *A "Petite Loge."* These small private boxes at the theater could be curtained off and were often used for love trysts. The Metropolitan Museum of Art, New York. Harris Brisbane Dick Fund, 1933 (34.22.1)

discerning society in the world.

Then once again her life was turned upside down. There were quarrels with her fellow actors and with the current First Gentleman. She tried, and failed, to get an order from the King making it legal for actors to marry. So she left Paris for a while, visited Voltaire, played opposite him in his theater at Ferney, came back to Paris, listened to bad advice, and at the age of forty-two, retired with a pension of a thousand livres a year ($3,000). After that she played only a few more times— twice for the court and on a few occasions in the private theater of her friend the duchesse de Ville- roy. The career of the century's greatest actress was over.

The bad advice came from her lover, M. de Valbelle. This promising and rich young man always managed to overspend. Clairon, who truly loved him, always gave him money; then, because he thought himself too good for an actress, he persuaded her to retire. For a while she remained in fashion. In 1772 she made a great impression when she gave a supper at the end of which a cur- tain opened, showing a bust of Voltaire. Stand- ing up, Mlle Clairon recited an ode to the great man, then crowned his marble head with a laurel wreath. Away at Ferney Voltaire nearly died of plea- sure; in Paris everyone talked about the evening.

Fashionable though she was, Clairon's money problems grew steadily more acute. Her looks faded early, and she no longer found rich lovers. Valbelle was merrily eating every penny she had saved, so in 1773, once again all her possessions were sold. They make a curious list: a female mummy in its case, wild men's shoes, Chinese masks, one parasol of feathers from the mogul's ostriches, shoes and silk stockings that had belonged to a famous dwarf—as well as engravings, jewelry, porcelain, an *écritoire* of gold-mounted crystal, a watch, a lorgnette. The proceeds of the sale came to the respectable sum of 23,496 livres ($70,000), and Clairon realized that she no longer loved Valbelle.

Anyone else would have been finished, but it happened that a German prince, the margrave of Anspach, came to Paris because he was tired of his sickly wife and his boring little court. This ugly but intelligent, kind, and sensitive man met Clairon and fell in love with her. In 1774 he took her back to Anspach, set her up in a grand house where she was served by more than a dozen domestics, and treated her much the way Louis XV had treated Mme de Pompadour.

Clairon took to it all like a fish to water. She dabbled in politics, fancied herself a power, and corresponded with the French foreign minister. She felt that she had at last found her true, exalted level. At the same time, it was all rather dull, so she did her best to help a beginning actor, Larive, whom she had met before leaving for Anspach. She returned to Paris for visits as often as she could, freely admitting to her friends that she hated Germany and was just waiting until she was rich enough not to need the margrave anymore.

It is hard to say whether that time would ever have come. As it turned out, the margrave met a pretty, young, adventurous Englishwoman, Lady Craven, who was far more cultivated and amusing than the aging Clairon. When Lady Craven designed an English garden for his castle in 1786, the margrave hesitated no longer and sent Clairon packing.

Now, it seemed, she would simply retire gracefully. She bought herself a large and luxurious house outside Paris and settled down to a quiet old age. However, her plans, like those of many other people, were rudely interrupted by the Revolution. She was in no danger herself, but she lost all her money. There could be no question of returning to the stage, so she looked again for a rich lover. The wonder is that she found one.

She met M. de Staël, M. Necker's son-in-law, in 1792. Perhaps because Mlle Clairon seemed restful compared with his wife, perhaps because he had a taste for old ladies, M. de Staël fell in love with the sixty-nine-year-old actress. True to form, she promptly got money out of him. In the summer of 1793 she was writing him: "Although I am ready to succumb under the weight of my years, of my infirmities, of the most terrible poverty, my heart has remained as sensitive as ever. Each of your sentences has changed the bitter tears I have been shedding for so long into sweet relief." As for Mme de Staël, who

knew and approved of the liaison, she even went so far as to consult Clairon about *Jane Grey,* a play she had just written, while, at regular intervals, M. de Staël paid up.

Trouble came in 1801, when M. de Staël's debts caught up with him and his wife refused to rescue him as she had always done before. On M. Necker's advice, she demanded and was granted a legal separation, so M. de Staël stopped supporting Clairon. He had legally bound himself to provide her with a yearly income, however, and she sued and won. Everything he owned was seized, including the bed he was lying in at the moment. Within less than a year, he died in poverty.

Even then, Mlle Clairon didn't give up. She persuaded Mme de Staël to talk Lucien Bonaparte, Napoleon's brother, into giving her a larger pension. Indefatigably she started looking for a new lover, and one can hardly help speculating on whom she might have bagged. As it was, she ran out of time. In January, 1803, quite forgotten— but not so poor—she caught a bad cold. By the end of the month the great Mlle Clairon was dead, and then memories revived to praise the woman who had invented modern acting.

Madame du Barry

To many, Mlle Clairon's rise to fame and relative fortune had seemed amazing, but soon her accomplishments paled before the career of an angelic-looking blond who became the uncrowned queen of France.

Perhaps because the French don't think much of people who are simply nice, Mme du Barry has had a rather bad press. She spent a lot of money, of course, but a number of museums would be markedly emptier today if she hadn't. She did start life as a deluxe prostitute (how else was a pretty girl to earn a living?), but when she was given the chance, she was faithful to the same man for sixteen years. Above all, she was kind: to her rich lovers, to Louis XV, to the poor in her neighborhood, to almost everyone at court, including the people who were saying dreadful things about her.

Mme du Barry did have one attribute about which everybody agreed: she was dazzlingly beautiful. It was almost impossible for a man to see her and not be moved. Colleval, one of her visitors, wrote:

> She was nonchalantly sitting, or rather lying, in a big armchair and wore a white dress with pink garlands which I can never forget. Madame du Barry, one of the prettiest women in a court where beauties were legion, was the most seductive of all because of the perfection of her entire person. Her hair, which she often dressed without powder, was the most beautiful blond, and so abundant that she hardly knew what to do with it. Her wide-open blue eyes had a frank and caressing look. . . . Her nose was adorable, her mouth very small, and her skin of a dazzling whiteness.

What Colleval doesn't say is that her bust was famous, and frequently displayed by deeply décolleté dresses.

All through Jeanne du Barry's life, her face and her figure were her fortune. The illegitimate daughter of a seamstress, Anne Bécu, and a monk, she was born in Lorraine in 1743. Six years later

her mother, from whom Jeanne evidently inherited her looks, was being kept by a rich army supplier who married her off (it was more respectable) and put the child in a Paris convent—an unfashionable one, of course. There the little girl received a fairly good education, so that when she was fifteen and it was time to leave, she was promptly hired as a companion by the widow of a *fermier-général,* Mme de la Garde.

The next two years were easy: Jeanne was charming, the old lady undemanding. Mme de la Garde had many men visitors who were struck by the companion's beauty. Soon they came to see the young girl, not downstairs in the drawing room, but upstairs in her bedroom. And since Jeanne's heart was tender, the traffic became so heavy that Mme de la Garde noticed it and fired her companion.

What next? For such a pretty girl, it was no problem. She became a *demoiselle de modes,* a salesgirl in a shop selling fashionable women's accessories. The pay wasn't much and the work was hard, but then there were the nights. Attractive *demoiselles de modes* never lacked for smart young lovers, and once again Jeanne was too kind to deny herself to anyone who asked. In a world of quick and plentiful affairs, she was known for the extraordinary number of men with whom she slept. In the eighteenth century, however, this seemed alluring, if anything.

Jeanne's stepfather had done business with a comte du Barry, a man of good family, but so wild and so dishonest that he was held in general contempt. By 1765 du Barry, who needed money, remembered the pretty Jeanne. He hated to see a good thing go to waste, so he fetched the twenty-year-old girl and installed her in his apartment. From then on Jeanne became du Barry's "milch cow," as a police report put it. He recruited clients, and they paid him a great deal of money to sleep with his pretty protégée. In return, she enjoyed a luxurious, idle life and a chance to meet some of the lesser intellectuals—Crébillon, Moncrif, and Collé, who came for supper and taught her how to hold her own in a salon. More important, she also entertained a long list of great nobles, headed by the maréchal de Richelieu, who

Drouais. *Mme du Barry.*
The Metropolitan Museum of Art, New York.
Harris Brisbane Dick Fund, 1954 (54.533.7)

Torch holder in the style of Pajou. One of a pair of life-size sculptures bearing the likeness of Mme du Barry, this torch holder was part of the decoration of Louveciennes. The Metropolitan Museum of Art, New York. Gift of J. Pierpont Morgan, 1906 (07.225.195)

was elderly now but still running after every pretty woman in sight. Soon she had learned how to speak and behave in society.

"Although," Talleyrand wrote some years later, "Madame de Pompadour was brought up and lived in the financial society of Paris, which was then rather distinguished, she had common manners, vulgar ways of speaking. . . . Madame du Barry . . . , although less well brought up, always managed to speak correctly. . . . She liked to talk and had caught the art of telling stories rather amusingly." Paradoxically, the girl who had once spent the night with anyone for a louis (24 livres) now gave the impression of having been to the manor born. And of course, there was always her dazzling beauty. The comte d'Espinchal, a connoisseur who saw her one night in her box at the Opéra, said, "I have never in my life seen anyone more attractive than this celestial person." Soon Jeanne, who although unmarried was calling herself du Barry, had become all the rage: you couldn't be in fashion if you hadn't had her, and to have her, you had to pay the comte a pretty fee.

Though this was all very well, there was one man in France who paid better than the rest and was more powerful besides. He frequently changed the girls with whom he slept, so there was no great future in the liaison, but still. . . . Under the pretext of visiting a minister, Jeanne went to Versailles and was introduced (probably by the maréchal de Richelieu) to Lebel, the King's confidential valet. Lebel, who was duly impressed, told the King. Anyone who was decently dressed could enter the palace's state apartments, so Louis XV gave Jeanne a good stare as he passed down the Hall of Mirrors. He agreed with Lebel and arranged a meeting with her outside the palace, where no one would know. Du Barry, of course, was delighted; so was Richelieu; and they both sat back to await the end of the affair and its consequent rewards.

As it turned out, they had done better than they dared hope. Louis XV, that great consumer of women, had always been a little in awe of famous beauties, but this one was easy, sweet, undemanding, and thoroughly experienced in bed.

LE BAIN.

De la Lettre ou du Chocolat   J'ai le cœur bien plus délicat

Que préfère Madame? Ah ma chére Justine,   Plus foible infiniment, hélas! que la poitrine.

Freudeberg. *The Bath*. Like the two gouaches by Baudoin (see following pages), this engraving reflects the kind of voluptuous enticement expected from women such as Mme du Barry in the early part of her career. The Metropolitan Museum of Art, New York. Harris Brisbane Dick Fund, 1933 (33.56.32)

The King, who was fifty-eight, found himself rejuvenated by Jeanne's face, figure, and little tricks. To everyone's surprise, du Barry's brother, who was luckily unmarried, appeared from the Languedoc on September 1, 1768, wedded Jeanne Bécu, and went back to his province. The marriage contract contained a number of unusual clauses. It specified that the groom had no control over the bride's fortune and that the bride under-took to support the groom: things could hardly have been clearer. As for the new comtesse du Barry, she must have enjoyed her wedding, especially since the priest turned out to be her own father.

In December, Jeanne was given rooms in Versailles near the King's own; it had become obvious that she was no mere fling. Still, no one thought that she could ever be presented at court.

Baudoin. *Morning*. The Metropolitan Museum of Art, New York.
Gift of Anne Payne Blumenthal, 1943 (43.163.19)

Baudoin. *Night*. The Metropolitan Museum of Art, New York.
Gift of Anne Payne Blumenthal, 1943 (43.163.20)
These slightly erotic gouaches, fashionable in France at the
time, show a young woman behaving very much like Mme
du Barry before she moved to Versailles.

The King himself knew what the comtesse's past had been.

"I'm told that I am Sainte-Foix's successor," he remarked to the duc de Noailles.

"Yes, Sire," the duke replied, "just as Your Majesty is Pharamond's successor," Pharamond, according to legend, being the first French king who had ruled some thousand years earlier.

Even without a presentation, it was all bad enough, the courtiers said. That little whore was actually living in the palace. Worse, she had imported her sister-in-law, Chon du Barry, as a sort of lady-in-waiting and had begun to receive a few wellborn women. For example, she entertained the maréchale de Mirepoix—whose gambling debts were such, Mme du Deffand acidly pointed out, that she would make friends with anybody in the hope that the King would prove generous.

Then, like a great thunderclap, came the news that Madame la comtesse du Barry was to be presented officially on April 22, 1769. The reaction was immediate. On one side were all the courtiers whose aristocratic pride was offended, joined by the duc de Choiseul, who feared for his influence and was egged on by his sister, the duchesse de Gramont (herself a disappointed postulant for the office of *maîtresse déclarée*). On the other was a small coterie led by the maréchal de Richelieu and his relative, the duc d'Aiguillon. Richelieu, of course, was in seventh heaven. After all the years of fighting uselessly against Mme de Pompadour, he would finally become the favorite's favorite—the new Choiseul, in fact. D'Aiguillon, of whom Mme du Barry appeared to be fond, and who had similar ambitions, shared in the rejoicing. The battle lines were drawn all the more clearly because Choiseul had decided to get rid of her before he even knew how Mme du Barry felt about him. Accordingly, he financed a series of obscene songs and pamphlets which featured detailed descriptions of du Barry's effect on the King's failing sexual powers. Imitators issued watered-down versions; here, for instance, is a song that was widely distributed in Paris and Versailles:

Vous connaissez, je crois, celle qu'à notre cour
On soutenait n'avoir jamais été cruelle . . .

Qui dans Paris ne connaît ses appâts?
Du laquais au marquis, chacun se souvient d'elle.

("You know, I think, the one whom at our court/ Was held never to have been cruel . . . / Who, in Paris, has not tasted her charms?/ From footman to marquis, all remember her well.") Curiously, the nasty little song was right: Jeanne was never cruel. That made her unique at Versailles, and it was one of the things the King liked about her.

Just as Louis XV and Mme de Pompadour had known why they were in love year after year, now the King and Mme du Barry knew why she had become the favorite. He wanted a lovely and very sexy woman who amused and soothed him and who never bothered him with political problems. She wanted fame, luxury, glamour, and an easy relationship with the King. As for politics, or indeed anything else that was serious, she neither understood it nor cared about it.

Her good will was universal. Jeanne was a genuinely kind person who was lucky enough to be living the dream of every Frenchwoman. By the spring of 1769, she had to all intents and purposes become the first lady in the world's most luxurious court. Her dresses were all the more dazzling in that they were adorned with diamonds: one bodice thickly covered with stones was in itself worth over 450,000 livres. Her apartments in the various royal palaces were newly decorated by the greatest artisans, and she was rapidly filling them with a sumptuous array of furniture made by *ébénistes* of genius. She rode about in gilded carriages. Best of all, she bought—avidly, ceaselessly—more and more jewels.

Perhaps because there was something appealing about her honest greed, perhaps because she never tried to assemble a coterie and become a real power, Louis XV was unusually generous with her. He gave her an annual pension of 1,200,000 livres, to which he added a separate, irrevocable income of 150,000 livres a year. Moreover, the favorite was able to draw on the treasury for all her household expenses. The King also presented her with the little château of Louveciennes—although he kept ownership of the ground so that the estate would revert to the crown on the favor-

Fan. Mother-of-pearl and silk on paper. No woman in the eighteenth century would have been caught without her fan. This simple accessory could become a jeweled, painted masterpiece. The Metropolitan Museum of Art, New York. From the Collection of Ella Wolcott Clark Rogers, Gift of Ella Mabel Clark, 1948 (48.58.5)

ite's death. The building itself was pleasant enough, but by the time Mme du Barry had finished decorating, it had become a jewel box crammed with marble, gilded bronze, carved boiseries, and exquisite furniture—for a further cost of over a million livres.

In one respect, at least, Jeanne resembled her predecessor, Mme de Pompadour: she loved porcelain. Besides buying vases, plates, and cups, she developed a taste for furniture covered with Sèvres porcelain plaques. By 1774 her collection was second only to the King's.

Also like Mme de Pompadour, Jeanne patronized artists, though she proved to have a rather undiscriminating eye. Her favorite portraitist, Drouais, is a competent, second-class painter who cannot compare with Van Loo, La Tour, or Boucher. Worse, she rejected a series of panels she had ordered from Fragonard, perhaps the greatest painter of the century, because she didn't find

them modern enough. (Today we are lucky to be able to admire them at the Frick Collection in New York.) The replacements, which she commissioned from Hubert Robert, were modish but distinctly inferior in quality. If her eye for painting was insensitive, at least she understood decoration: it was an essential part of that luxurious atmosphere she loved so much and was so skilled at creating.

Of course, there could be no grand life without servants. This former salesgirl had more than fifty footmen and, counting cooks, coachmen, gardeners, maids, and butlers, employed well over a hundred servants. Zamor, the little black page who followed her everywhere, had a series of specially made suits. For example, there was a hussar's costume with silver braid, a little saber, and a plumed bonnet. His other ensembles, including a sailor suit, were flesh colored, blue, pink, silver, and white, in silk, taffeta, and velvet. Zamor's

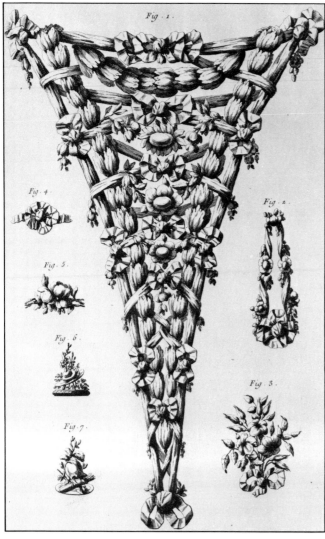

Diamond bodice, a plate from the *Encyclopédie* representing a diamond-covered bodice similar to the one given by Louis XV to Mme du Barry and valued at over 450,000 livres ($1.5 million). Thomas J. Watson Library, The Metropolitan Museum of Art, New York

clothes cost the countess more than 6,000 livres a year—an adequate income for a middle-class family.

It was a good thing that taste in the eighteenth century seems to have been innate. Otherwise one suspects that Mme du Barry would have bought hideous objects with equal enthusiasm, as long as they were valuable. What mattered to her was ownership of vast quantities of the very best there was—which in the 1770s was very good indeed.

By the side of her bed, she had two large gold candlesticks adorned with silver doves. When she ordered her table silver, the court jeweler made twelve dozen of everything. Over the six-year period from 1768 to 1774, she spent more than 600,000 livres on silks and lace alone. She ran up a bill of 170,000 livres with a coming young dress designer, Mlle Bertin, who was by no means her principal couturiere. At a time when a well-to-do noble family could live luxuriously on 30,000 livres a year, Mme du Barry spent that amount on the upkeep of her horses and carriages. And although the King was constantly giving her jewels, she ran up 2 million livres' worth of jewelers' bills. As a result, her collection was as fabulous as it was famous. Besides the diamond bodice and a diamond necklace of spectacular proportions, she owned over 140 large diamonds, 700 smaller ones, 300 very large pearls, 3 enormous sapphires, and 7 huge and renowned emeralds, as well as a plethora of lesser stones and gold jewelry, boxes, and toilette utensils.

Unlike jewels in modern settings, precious stones in the eighteenth century were mounted so that the same diamond, for instance, could be used in a coiffure as the agrafe for a feather, in a necklace as the central stone, or on a bracelet; it could even be sewn onto a skirt. Large stones were often set singly, smaller ones combined into a motif—such as a curlicue, which could be blended with other motifs. Instead of owning many necklaces or bracelets, Mme du Barry collected stones which she could use in any way she saw fit at any particular moment. In fact, women often wore all their best jewelry as part of a splendid court dress. Where designers would use rhinestones today, Mme du Barry used diamonds.

The look of eighteenth-century stones was different, too. They had fewer facets, so that they seemed less brilliant than modern jewels. There were strict rules about the settings: diamonds, for instance, were always mounted in silver, which was thought to look best with them. Colored stones, on the other hand, were set in gold and, unless they were spectacular, were supposed to be worn only during the day.

Her wealth, combined with the King's interest, was more than enough to keep Mme du Barry satisfied, but this idyll was marred by the enmity of the duc de Choiseul. Because the anti-Choiseul coterie was desperate to use the favorite, the prime minister chose to believe that the countess was working against him. Nothing could have been further from the truth. Mme du Barry wanted only to be tolerated: she even had Louis XV invite Choiseul to a reconciliation supper at Bellevue in March, 1769, but the duke could not be pacified. Kaunitz, the Austrian ambassador, was also rabidly anti—du Barry because he feared that the Austrian alliance might not survive Choiseul's dismissal. The man whose fulsome praise of Mme de Pompadour was cited in Chapter 2 wrote of du Barry: "It is . . . scandalous to see the maréchal de Richelieu and to hear . . . the Governor and the Governess of the Royal Children . . . say publicly that God allows this evil to cure a greater evil; and this greater evil, according to them, is the existence of M. de Choiseul."

It was true that the ultra-Catholic party, who loathed Choiseul because he was a freethinker, had formed an alliance with the new and scandalous mistress. This comical partnership was attended by utter lack of success for the Catholics. In June, 1770, Louis XV wrote the prime minister: "You take good care of the affairs of State. I am pleased with you. But watch out for your entourage and those who are always ready with advice; I have always hated those people and detest them now more than ever. You know Mme du Barry. . . . She is pretty, I am pleased with her. . . . She has no hatred for you; she knows your intelligence and does not wish you ill. . . . She is very pretty and pleases me. Let that suffice." Still Choiseul kept up his war against the favorite; still the

The Emperor of China. Gold, enamel, and precious stones. Hair ornament. Photograph courtesy of A La Vieille Russie, New York

pamphlets poured forth in spite of anything that Jeanne could do.

Suddenly, on December 23, 1770, Choiseul was dismissed and exiled. Naturally everyone assumed it was Mme du Barry's doing, and she was attacked in consequence. In fact, she had had nothing to do with it. Choiseul, who was thoroughly infatuated with his own talents, had simply been about to start a war with England against the King's express orders. Besides, he had sided with the Parlements, a selfish and reactionary plutocracy, in their fight against a whole train of reforms which (if Louis XVI had not canceled them in 1774) might well have saved the monarchy. Mme du Barry was delighted with Choiseul's dismissal, of course. Her friend the duc d'Aiguillon was made a minister, and she was glad to see the King becoming more relaxed. Just then, however, she was far more interested in a new dress of white striped satin, pleated with gold in the shape of rippling water and adorned with garlands of ruby-

Drouais. *Mme du Barry.*
National Gallery of Art,
Washington, D.C. Timken Collection

90

Fragonard. *The Meeting*. This is one of the panels commissioned by Mme du Barry from Fragonard and rejected in favor of a more fashionable set of paintings by Hubert Robert. Copyright The Frick Collection, New York

enameled gold spangle bouquets.

Now everything went Jeanne's way; even the pro-Choiseul Mme du Deffand admitted that the countess was extraordinarily pretty, and not a bad girl besides. Everything, that is, except for the hostility of a slip of a girl, the new Dauphine. The young Marie Antoinette, partly through chance, had fallen in with the little group of elderly, bigoted women around the King's daughters. This clique hated the favorite for two good reasons: she was attractive, and she caused Louis XV to sin. Then too, Marie Antoinette regretted the loss of Choiseul, the architect of her marriage to the Dauphin. On every occasion she cut Mme du Barry dead; soon, of course, everyone had noticed. The poor good-tempered countess begged the King to stop this constant humiliation; the King called in the Austrian ambassador; the ambassador spoke to the Dauphine; but still the favorite was greeted by icy silence. Finally Maria Theresa wrote her daughter a long, stern letter. On January 1, 1772, as Mme du Barry curtsyed before the Dauphine, she heard a reluctant voice say, "There are many people at Versailles today, Madame." Within minutes everyone in the palace had heard the news, and henceforth the favorite reigned uncontested.

Marie Antoinette had her revenge after May 10, 1774, when Louis XV died of smallpox. The Dauphine became Queen, and Mme du Barry was sent off to a rather bleak convent in the provinces. The ex-favorite endured her boredom without complaint, however, and after two years all was forgiven. She was allowed to go back to wonderful Louveciennes, and there she lived, beautiful as ever, in contented splendor until the Revolution. She was even happy in love—with the duc de Brissac, who was tall, handsome, kind, and married to a sickly woman whom he never saw. Soon he and Mme du Barry formed a united couple. She won wide acceptance in society; even Emperor Joseph II, Marie Antoinette's brother, made a point of visiting her when he came through Paris.

In 1786 the duc de Brissac decided to commission a portrait of the countess. Naturally he asked Mme Vigée-Lebrun, whose work was immensely fashionable, and the painter repaired to Louveciennes. Mme du Barry, she wrote,

. . . received me in the most gracious style. She seemed to have excellent manners, but I found her wit more easy than her politeness. Her glance was that of a coquette: her large eyes were never completely open and her speech had a childish quality which no longer befitted her age. . . . Winter and summer she wore only robes of white percale or muslin and every day, no matter what the weather was like, she went for a walk. . . .

At night, we were most often alone by the fire, Mme du Barry and I. She sometimes talked about Louis XV and his court, always with the greatest respect for the one and the greatest kindness for the other, but she always avoided giving details. . . . [Otherwise] her conversation was usually quite dull. She was kind in both word and deed, and was immensely helpful to [the village of] Louveciennes where all the poor received charity from her. . . .

Every day after dinner, we went and had coffee in that pavilion which was so famous for the taste and richness of its ornamentation. The first time Mme du Barry showed it to me, she said, "It is in this room that Louis XV did me the honor of being my guest at dinner." . . . The salon was ravishing, one saw the most beautiful views from it, and the mantelpieces, the doors were all adorned in the most dazzling way; the locks were as admirable as the greatest masterpieces of jewelry and the furniture was of a richness and elegance beyond all description.

It was not Louis XV, then, who sat on those magnificent sofas but the duc de Brissac.

The Revolution, when it came, didn't bother the countess. She was as little interested in politics as ever, and her only comment during a series of riots was, "If Louis XV had lived, he never would have allowed all this to happen." Still, she didn't see why it should affect her. Even when the people turned violent in 1790–91, she calmly pointed out that she was no aristocrat and therefore in no danger. Besides, she had always been charitable and was widely loved in her district.

Then, in January, 1791, while she was spending the night in Paris, her house was broken into and her jewels stolen. It turned out that the thieves were led by a soldier who had been placed in the house, at Mme du Barry's own request, as a guard against random violence. It was a tremendous loss, of course. Besides the fact that she loved her diamonds, jewels represented the bulk of her fortune—some 1.5 million livres. Still, she didn't panic, and when the jewels turned up in London the following month, she got a passport and crossed the Channel.

It was a complicated matter. Proof was needed in England, where the thieves and the diamonds had come to rest. But the theft had taken place in France, and the new Revolutionary courts felt no great sympathy for the ex-favorite.

All through 1791 and the first half of 1792, the countess kept traveling back and forth, always making sure that she would not be considered an émigrée. Otherwise she ignored the Revolution. But in September, 1792, her lover, the duc de Brissac, who had commanded the King's guard, was massacred in Versailles as he was being transferred from a jail in Orléans to a jail in Paris. Within an hour the screaming mob bearing the duke's head on a pike invaded the park at Louveciennes, broke the window, and threw the grisly remains at Mme du Barry's feet.

Apparently the tender Jeanne was also shallow: she managed to recover from the dreadful scene in a matter of days and went right on trying to get her jewels back. Perhaps, after all, she had learned selfishness from her life at Versailles. Late in September, with a passport signed by the foreign minister himself, she returned to London. While she was gone, she was denounced as an émigrée by Zamor, once her little black page, now her footman. Zamor hoped to get his hands on the contents of Louveciennes by having the countess arrested. Undaunted, Mme du Barry returned to France, fought for her estate, and, amazingly, won.

This was in May, 1793. France was living under the Reign of Terror, but the ex-favorite saw no reason why anything should happen to her. Then Zamor denounced her again, and on July 1, she was arrested. She complained so vigorously, however, that she was set free. It was a unique case, for she received the unanimous support of the inhabitants of Louveciennes. On August 9,

Hubert Robert. *Visitors Leaving a Prison.* This is a view of the prison where Mme du Barry was held before and during her trial. The Metropolitan Museum of Art, New York. Bequest of Anne D. Thomson, 1923 (23.280.6)

the dread Committee for General Safety actually exonerated her with the statement, "There is no accusation that can legitimately be made against the citizeness Du Barry." And the triumphant Jeanne spent an idyllic summer with her new lover, the duc de Rohan-Chabot.

It would have been paradoxical indeed if the ex-favorite had come through the Revolution unscathed. But on September 22, 1793, she was denounced again by another greedy servant, rearrested, and this time, despite all her protests, detained in jail. In December she was tried as a British spy. The accusation was grotesque, but it sufficed. Just in case anyone had forgotten, the public accuser told the jury: "You have before you this Lais [a legendary prostitute of the fourth century B.C.], famous for the corruption of her life, the publicity and fame of her debauchery. . . . You need not pay attention to the scandal and opprobrium of her elevation, the turpitude and shame of her infamous prostitution." This was like telling a bull not to pay attention to the red rag. That night at eleven, Mme du Barry was condemned to die.

The next morning, at the hour when she was to be taken to her execution, she made a desperate bid to save her life by revealing the hiding places in the park of Louveciennes where she had secreted the rest of her fortune. It didn't help, of course. At four the cart came for her, and this woman who had fought so courageously now broke down. She cried, sobbed, and shouted incoherently, but still she was dragged off. When she finally reached the Place de la Révolution, she had to be carried up the steps by the executioner. She lay there half dead for a minute; then the blade fell and a dreadful, shrill cry sounded over the crowd. The pretty Jeanne, that morsel fit for a king, had finally paid for her crime.

Carlin (signed by). *Lady's desk.* Decorated with Sèvres porcelain plaques. Tulipwood, walnut, and harewood veneered on oak. This desk, or an identical one, belonged to Mme du Barry and was part of the furniture at Louveciennes. The Metropolitan Museum of Art, New York. Gift of Samuel H. Kress Foundation, 1958 (58.75.49)

Gilbert Stuart. *Abigail Adams.* National Gallery of Art, Washington, D.C. Gift of Mrs. Robert Homans

In Search of Freedom

Abigail Adams

Georgiana,
   Duchess of Devonshire

When the American Colonies rose against King George, it was obvious to smart people in France that they were watching the birth of a new Roman republic. Ancient Rome was all the fashion, and the comparison was inevitable. The Americans, like the early Romans, were industrious, honest, and pure. And a number of prominent Americans seemed to fit the historical pattern. George Washington, like Cincinnatus, led his countrymen to victory and then, without any thought of self-aggrandizement, went back to his "farm" at Mount Vernon. And while Martha Washington was perhaps a little too grand for the part of Mrs. Cincinnatus, the second First Lady—and before that, the first Second Lady—of the Republic, Abigail Adams, seemed to embody the greatness of spirit, the practicality, and the toughness of those famous Roman matrons who, in their day, had helped to save their city.

Like Mme Necker, Mrs. Adams's ambition was bound up in her husband's career. Like Mme Necker, she was a devoted wife. But luckily for her, John Adams towered above Jacques Necker and needed no one to fabricate a reputation for him. Instead of a well-organized conspiracy, the Adamses' marriage was a partnership—so much so, in fact, that John got into trouble because he had written Abigail telling her (a woman!) exactly what was happening in politics. And for several years it was the husband, staying in Philadelphia, who depended upon the wife in Massachusetts for news of the war, since Massachusetts was the front.

Abigail was born in 1744 in Weymouth, Massachusetts, to the Reverend and Mrs. William Smith. Financially the Smiths were comfortable but not rich; still, it was impossible to be more respectable or respected. Mrs. Smith had been a Quincy—one of the best and most politically active families in the Colony. The Smiths' house was spacious and full of books, and since Abigail, a bright and cheerful child, was also delicate,

Russell. *Abigail Adams*. Photograph courtesy of The Society for the Preservation of New England Antiquities, Boston, Massachusetts

her father decided to educate her himself. He did a good job: by the time she was seventeen Abigail had read widely—in Molière, Locke, and all the English poets, among others. She could also cook, sew, and keep house. Altogether, she was quite a catch, and when John Adams met her, he wrote a friend that she was the best-educated woman he had ever known.

The instant Miss Smith and Mr. Adams came together, it was obvious that they were very much alike. They seemed made for each other; still, their courtship lasted for three years. John was twenty-nine, Abigail just two and a half weeks short of her twentieth birthday, when they were married and moved to the farm John had inherited in Braintree. Neither had much money. Adams was a young lawyer of rising repute and radical inclinations. He had belonged to a small group, composed mostly of lawyers, that had fruitlessly fought against the Writs of Assistance and the searches for contraband that they authorized. As it turned out, this struggle was only a rehearsal, a stand taken on libertarian issues that was eventually carried to its logical conclusion.

John and Abigail's honeymoon was happy, their new life harmonious. The two young people were bright and talkative; they held identical political views; and they were very much in love. Abigail enjoyed her sturdy house, built some twenty years earlier, with its big central brick chimney, weathered, unpainted clapboard exterior, and added "leanter" (lean-to) containing the kitchen and dining room. The house was comfortable but not at all grand. Downstairs there was a parlor, John's study-office, with its own door to the outside, and the two rooms in the leanter. Upstairs there were two large bedrooms and a tiny one, along with a maid's room in the attic. Outside were fields, cows, and farm animals. The young couple worked hard, Abigail at keeping house, John in the fields as well as at his law practice. Within the first month they established a pattern: every day John emptied the wallet, which contained his fees, into Abigail's purse, and she managed the family finances. Jean Jacques Rousseau, who believed in the virtues of a life spent close to nature, love, and fidelity, would have been ecstatic.

In 1765 John was one of the leaders in the movement against the Stamp Act, a tax imposed by the British Parliament on the Colonies without their consent. His resolution against the act was adopted by the town meeting of Braintree and widely circulated along the eastern seaboard. He was gathering political support while putting his career on the line, but once again the battle was lost.

Abigail fully shared in the fight. Like John, she believed in liberty, and she had already become his trusted partner and adviser. This, however, was only one of her many occupations. She continued to read and to learn. She bore a daughter in 1765 and a son, John Quincy, in 1767.

Copley. *John Adams*. Photograph courtesy of the Harvard University Portrait Collection, Bequest Ward Nicholas Boylston in 1828, Fogg Art Museum, Cambridge, Massachusetts

The Bostonians Paying the Excise Man. Numerous cartoons relating to the Revolutionary War were published in the seventies. The Metropolitan Museum of Art, New York. Charles Allen Munn Collection, Bequest of Charles Allen Munn, 1924 (24.90.32)

Like her parents, she educated her children at home.

Soon, however, "home" was no longer a farm: although the Adamses kept their Braintree property, they moved to Boston. John had become too successful, too busy to live out of town. Of course, he still rode circuit; and it was then that he wrote Abigail: "Let us therefore, my dear partner, apply ourselves by every way we can to the cultivation of our farm. Let frugality and industry be our virtues. . . . And above all the cares of this life, let our ardent anxiety be to mould the minds and manners of our children."

The political situation, however, was deteriorating rapidly. John and Abigail were in agreement that the British must be resisted, and organizing that resistance took more and more of their time. Meeting followed meeting at their house in Brattle Square, and Abigail attended all of them. Then the British under Governor Gage oc-

cupied Boston in force. Finally John went off to the Continental Congress in Philadelphia, and Abigail, who moved back to Braintree, was left to manage house, farm, children, servants, crops, and livestock. Busy as she was, she could never grow accustomed to the worst of her sacrifices: her separation from her husband.

As it turned out, that separation immeasurably enriched our understanding of the Revolutionary period. The letters exchanged between husband and wife are not just literate and lively; they give us a vivid account of events in the two places that mattered most: Boston and Philadelphia.

Abigail's first letter is dated August 19, 1774. She wrote:

> The great distance between us makes the time appear very long to me. The great anxiety I feel for my country, for you and for our family renders the day tedious and the night unpleasant. The rock and quick sands appear on every side. . . . Did any kingdom or state regain its liberty when once it was invaded, without bloodshed? I cannot think of it without horror. Yet we are told that all the misfortunes of Sparta were occasioned by their too great solicitude for their present tranquillity. . . . They ought to have reflected, says Polybius, that "there is nothing more shameful, and, at the same time, more pernicious when attained by bad measures and purchased at the price of liberty."

In France a woman helped govern the state; in America a woman was sharing the danger and summoning the resolution necessary to shape a new order.

Naturally, Mrs. Adams took a firmly partisan view of the rebellion. The Tories were villains, and it was with glee that, on September 14, 1774, she wrote about their discomfiture: "Not a Tory but hides his head. The Church parson thought they [the Patriots] were coming after him and ran up a garret; they say another jumped out of his window and hid among the corn while a third crept up under his board fence and told his beads." We can hear her laughing now.

Life in Braintree was not usually so amusing, though; and as the days passed, it grew rapidly more precarious. The British troops were more violent, the harbor was closed to shipping, commerce came to an end. Manufactured goods had been imported from England, so paint, cloth, sugar, tools, even needles and thread, were no longer available. Abigail's children and servants must be fed and clothed, she had to supervise the planting and reaping, and she complained bitterly about the huge wages she had to offer because she had not yet understood that the Continental paper currency was actually worth less than the old metal coins. There was an epidemic of dysentery, and one of her maids died. Essential foods could no longer be purchased in Boston. There were cooking, sewing, weaving, repairs of all sorts, and lessons for the children. And always there were the letters to John in Philadelphia, where he was struggling to convince the Congress that independence must be achieved and that the war must be fought more efficiently.

Abigail never grew used to John's absence, although she did not reproach him for it. How could she? He was doing his duty; but she wrote, "I dare not express to you, at three hundred miles' distance, how ardently I long for your return." And things did not improve; in the spring of 1778 John was sent to Europe to obtain loans and arms. "'Tis a little more than three weeks," her letter said, "since the dearest of friends and tenderest of husbands left his solitary partner and quitted all the fond endearments of domestic felicity for the dangers of the sea." They had been married for fourteen years, and the love between them had only grown stronger.

The fact that Abigail was alone and lonely didn't mean that she couldn't manage. "I would not have you be distressed about me," she wrote in July, 1775. "Danger, they say, makes people valiant. Hitherto, I have been distressed but not dismayed. I have felt for my country and her sons. I have bled with them and for them." She had also assisted them, whether it meant feeding a troop of volunteers marching through Braintree or giving up her pewter spoons to be made into bullets. She also reported fully on the political and military situation in the area. Her letters were a powerful weapon for her husband. When Congress hesitated, John could point out, for instance: "The distresses of the inhabitants of Boston are beyond the power of language to describe; there are but very few who are permitted [by the English troops] to come out in a day; they delay giving passes, making them wait from hour to hour." The Americans were experiencing a new kind of combat: a war carried out by a colonial power against its own subjects. It tended to

Paul Revere. *A View of Boston.* I. N. Phelps Stokes Collection, Art, Prints and Photographs Division, The New York Public Library, Astor, Lenox and Tilden Foundations

be cruel, degrading, and above all, ineffective, since growing oppression only met with growing resistance.

All through the traumatic events of 1775 and 1776, Abigail did her work with undaunted courage, retaining a cool independence of judgment and encouraging her husband; she had no doubt that separation from England must come.

"I long to hear," she wrote in March, 1776, "that you have declared an independency." She went on to point out, clearly not for the first time, that women were just as good as men:

> And by the way, in the new code of laws which I suppose it will be necessary for you to make, I desire you would remember the ladies and be more favorable and generous to them than your ancestors. Do not put such unlimited power into the hands of husbands. Remember, all men would be tyrants if they could. If particular care and attention is not paid to the ladies, we are determined to foment a rebellion, and will not hold ourselves bound by any laws in which we have no voice or representation.
>
> That your sex is naturally tyrannical is a truth so thoroughly established as to admit of no dispute; but such of you as wish to be happy willingly give up the harsh title of master for the most tender and endearing one of friend. Why not, then, put it out of the power of the vicious and the lawless to use us with cruelty and indignity with impunity? Men of sense in all ages abhor those customs which treat us only as the vassals of your sex.

Her tone is sometimes jocular, but the underlying feeling is very serious. There can be no doubt that women, because they played such an essential role in the American Revolution, at the same time claimed and won a large measure of equality. In a huge, sparsely settled country, women had to cope with the same kinds of problems that men did. This was true whether the women were Nantucket fishermen's wives, whose husbands were at sea for months at a time; shop owners, who ran the business while their men were at war; or young girls who led free, unchaperoned lives.

However, in his answer John Adams treated the whole idea as a joke. Perhaps he felt that it was a question of custom, not law, since he had always considered Abigail an equal partner. Undaunted, she returned to the topic: "I cannot say that I think you are very generous to the ladies, for whilst you are proclaiming peace and good will to men, emancipating all nations, you insist upon retaining an absolute power over wives. But you must remember that arbitrary power is like most other things which are very hard, very liable to be broken."

Abigail was also concerned about slavery, which in 1776 was still legal in every state. In Boston the English were attempting to enlist black servants by promising them freedom. This, Abigail thought, would never do, since it was undermining the Patriots' efforts, and besides, keeping slaves was morally wrong. Clearly, one task of the new American government would be to abolish slavery. As it turned out, of course, the United States took quite a while to get around to that. But in Massachusetts, where John Adams had influence, slavery was abolished before the end of the Revolution.

Soon the fighting came close to Braintree. Abigail wrote her husband on March 2, 1776:

> I have been in a continual state of anxiety and expectation ever since you left me. It has been said "tomorrow" and "tomorrow" for this month, but when the dreadful tomorrow will be, I know not. But hark! The house this instant shakes with the roar of cannon.

Three days later she added:

> I went to bed about twelve and rose again a little after one. I could no more sleep than if I had been in the engagement; the rattling of the windows, the jar of the house, the continual roar of twenty-four pounders, and the bursting of shells . . . realise a scene to us of which we could form scarcely any conception.

In the course of the war there were good times as well as bad. In July, 1775, for instance, General Washington came to Massachusetts. John Adams had been one of his most enthusiastic backers in Congress; Abigail went to meet him and found him even more impressive than she had expected. Then there were John's rare visits to Braintree, when the couple felt great joy in being reunited even if it was only for a few weeks.

There were honors, too: for instance, the commonwealth made John its chief justice, a post he eventually had to decline owing to the press of his work for Congress. And of course, there was the Declaration of Independence. John Adams signed it, but it is to Abigail that we owe an account of its reception:

Last Thursday, after hearing a very good sermon, I went with the multitude into King Street to hear the Proclamation for Independence read. . . . The troops appeared under arms and all the inhabitants assembled there . . . when Colonel Crofts read from the balcony of the State House the Proclamation. Great attention was given to every word. As soon as he ended, the cry from the balcony was "God save our American states," and then three cheers which rent the air. The bells rang, the privateers fired, the forts and batteries, the cannon were discharged, the platoons followed, and every face appeared joyful. . . . After dinner, the King's arms were taken down from the State House . . . and burnt in King Street. Thus ends Royal authority in this state. And all the people shall say Amen.

John was then in Philadelphia. When he returned to Braintree, he stayed only a few weeks and left for Europe, taking John Quincy with him. A few days later Abigail heard that his ship had been sunk, and she spent several anguished weeks until she found that the news was false. And, once more, there were some pleasant moments. When Admiral d'Estaing subsequently arrived with the French fleet, he gave a great feast aboard his flagship in honor of Mrs. Adams. She enjoyed it all the more because he told her that he had found John Quincy "un jeune homme très gentil" ("a very nice young man"). John was able to send her some supplies: cloth, sugar, flour, cider. All too seldom for her, he sent letters too.

"It would be futile to attempt descriptions of this country [France]," he wrote. "The richness, the magnificence and splendor are beyond all description. . . . But what is all this to me? . . . I cannot help suspecting that the more elegance, the less virtue. . . . All the luxury I desire in the world is the company of my dearest friend and my children."

There was a brief respite from traveling in 1779, when John spent the entire summer in Braintree. He left again in November, and this time Abigail didn't see him for five years—a separation from which she suffered greatly. When they were finally reunited, it was because she had taken the six-week ocean voyage to Europe.

Having landed in England, Mrs. Adams loved what she saw: the roads were smooth, the inns clean and hospitable, the meals delicious. The enormous size of London almost confounded her, but she discovered that it was really like a superior Boston. She could feel at home there, although London had more variety than any American city. It was also more fashion conscious, of which Abigail disapproved even while she busily bought new clothes.

Then she was off to Paris, which she didn't much like. The streets were dirty and smelly, and while she grudgingly admitted that the buildings

The White House in 1820. It would require too many servants, Mrs. Adams complained. I. N. Phelps Stokes Collection, Art, Prints and Photographs Division, The New York Public Library, Astor, Lenox and Tilden Foundations

were handsome, she felt what would later become a typically American sense of amused superiority. Her house in Auteuil, she wrote, was very grand and quite beautifully decorated, but it was inconvenient and required too many servants, each of whom did his job and not one whit more. Besides, the French didn't know how to clean floors properly. You couldn't use water on parquet, so all they did was push the dust around. French manners, while rather good, were eccentric. Mrs. Adams could hardly believe, for instance, that men and women sat together at the dinner table instead of in facing rows. And with the exception of Mme de La Fayette, who was simple and kind, French ladies were overdressed and paid too much attention to fashion.

One can't help wondering what would have happened if Abigail had stayed a little longer. Her attitude was beginning to change by the time the Adamses moved to England, where John had become the first American minister to the Court of St. James. A new appreciation, for instance, was emerging in her view of the French ballet. As she wrote her sister:

> The dresses and beauty of the performers were enchanting, but no sooner did the dance commence but I felt my delicacy wounded, and I was ashamed to be seen to look at them. Girls clothed in the thinnest silk and gauze with their petticoats short, springing two feet from the floor, poising themselves in the air, with their feet flying and as perfectly showing their garters and drawers as though no petticoat had been worn, was a sight altogether new to me. Their motions are as light as air, and as quick as lightning; they balance themselves to astonishment. No description can equal the reality. . . . Shall I speak the truth and say that repeatedly seeing their dances has worn off that disgust which I at first felt, and that I see them now with pleasure?

There is no telling what further depravity Mrs. Adams might have discovered in herself if she had not sailed off to London in May, 1785.

She was surprised to find that after the French, English society seemed a bore, the court deadly, and Queen Charlotte odious. Abigail loved London itself, however. The people were kind and interesting, the streets clean, the houses conve-

nient. Hyde Park was a model for all parks, Mrs. Siddons an admirable actress. As for Handel's *Messiah,* she wrote: "I could scarcely believe myself an inhabitant of earth. I was one continued shudder from the beginning to the end of the performance."

With Paris and London, Mrs. Adams had come to the end of her heroic period. Even the turmoil of American politics could hardly compare with those early days in Massachusetts when it took such courage to oppose the English and so much sacrifice to achieve independence. Again, her life in France, that strange, sophisticated, and rather frightening country, had called upon new resources: running a farm in Braintree was no preparation for conducting a salon in Auteuil. Finally, she had met the challenge of London, where the wife of the first American minister must dress and behave as elegantly as an English noblewoman. It was important to prove decisively that civilization flourished across the Atlantic.

By the time the Adamses returned to the United States, Abigail's health was beginning to fail. Great events were still ahead of her, of course. John Adams, for two terms Washington's Vice President, became President himself under disputed and difficult circumstances. He was also the first American leader to be voted out of office. There was a lot of politics, a lot of criticism: Mrs. Adams, people said, told the President what to do; she was the power behind the throne. Of course it wasn't true. John consulted her as he had always done, but in the new White House (which, Abigail said, would require too many servants) as at the farm in Braintree, John and Abigail's partnership was one of equals.

The nation continued settled and prosperous as the great days of the Revolution faded into the past. When Abigail died in October, 1818, this had become a new kind of country. As they watched her coffin go past, the crowds knew that in Abigail Adams they had lost not only a woman of remarkable intelligence and courage, but also the embodiment of an earlier spirit. And indeed, more than a century passed before women again thought that men were, or should be, friends and equal partners.

Reynolds. *Georgiana, Duchess of Devonshire.* Huntington Library, Art Gallery and Botanical Gardens, San Marino, California

Georgiana, Duchess of Devonshire

During the American Revolution Abigail Adams of Braintree, Massachusetts, would have been surprised to learn that one of the greatest ladies in England, Georgiana, Duchess of Devonshire, shared her wishes for the Colonies' independence. The two women were also alike in that both were intelligent and well read. There the similarities ended, however. The Duchess was sophisticated, cosmopolitan, frivolous. She cared enormously about fashion. She lived in palaces and, though she was extremely rich, accumulated mountainous debts. Her relationship with her husband was one of convenience: unlike the Adamses, the Devonshires were never in love and remained acquaintances, really, rather than friends. Finally, although she took the American side during the war, it was less from personal conviction than because her family belonged to the closed and powerful circle of the great Whig aristocrats.

It is hard for us today to imagine what it meant to be a duchess in England during the eighteenth century. Unlike the French monarchy, England's royal family counted for very little. It was foreign (George I and George II were German), it was dowdy, and it was almost powerless. Since the death of Queen Anne in 1714, England had been ruled essentially by a Prime Minister and a cabinet supported by Parliament. That cabinet was made up of members of the great Whig families, who owned much of the country and had put the Hanoverians on the throne.

For the English aristocrats, this was the golden age when they were rich, glamorous, and powerful. The sense of awe they inspired lingers in Jane Austen's novels, even though these were written as England was beginning to change. Next to the aristocracy, the dreary court of George III paled; indeed, attending it was considered a great chore. Barons, viscounts, earls, and marquesses were very grand people indeed, and to be a duke or duchess was to have reached semidivine heights. Noblemen were called My Lord or Your Lordship; dukes were addressed as Your Grace—a title which, as recently as Elizabeth I's reign, had been used by the monarch.

It was in this aristocratic republic that Georgiana Spencer was born. The third Earl Spencer, her father (and an ancestor of Diana, Princess of Wales today), was a typical Whig—rich, opinionated, and fiercely independent. He had been born a Whig; his children were Whigs; they married other Whigs; it was a closed, comfortable society. Everyone knew that Tories survived here and there, but they had been out of power since Queen Anne's death and were not expected ever to matter again. Still, they were properly despised.

"Mama," asked the daughter of a famous Whig, "are Tories born wicked, or do they grow wicked afterwards?"

"They are born wicked and grow worse," was the reply.

With this monopoly of power went universal corruption. By virtue of his birth, for instance, Horace Walpole was given an ushership of the exchequer, a clerkship of the estreats, and comptrollership of the pipe. These offices, sinecures all, brought him the sizable income of £1,300 a year. Then there were the rotten boroughs which returned members of Parliament at the behest of the local landlord. Since majorities in the House of Commons had to be bought, the proprietorship of a borough was valuable indeed. Votes in Parliament were generally for sale. Sir Robert Walpole, the great Prime Minister and the father of Horace, said that he even had to bribe members to vote for their conscience.

Georgiana Spencer grew up talking politics. Together with her sister and brother, she was raised at Althorp, where she had been born in 1757. Her father, grandson of the great Duke of Marlborough, was hugely rich even by the standards of his time and milieu. Untypically, he was also happily married. The countess's sweetness was proverbial, and the children's lives were pleasant ones. Because their parents were cultivated, they received sound educations not only in history, mathematics, and literature, but also in French and Italian—and for the girls, in music and drawing as well.

Frye. *Queen Charlotte*. The Metropolitan Museum
of Art, New York. The Elisha Whittelsey Collection,
The Elisha Whittelsey Fund, 1969 (69.669.1)

In 1773 when Georgiana was almost sixteen, she went to Spa with her parents and met William, fifth Duke of Devonshire. She was lovely, wellborn, rich. He was a member of one of the very greatest English families and a landowner with holdings of hundreds of thousands of acres. He liked her and told Lord Spencer. The match was eminently suitable. In June, 1774, Lady Georgiana Spencer, to the envy of her contemporaries, became Duchess of Devonshire. The Spencers were thrilled, society approved, the Duke himself, though he was on the rebound from a previous romance, was pleased. Everyone found the match highly satisfactory, except the new Duchess.

Georgiana knew better than to disobey her parents, but in fact she was in love with the Duke of Hamilton. Although she made it plain to the

Duke of Devonshire that she came to him reluctantly, he could hardly have cared less: he himself was in love with the Countess of Derby.

Still, for a marriage of convenience, things seemed to go rather well at first. To the seventeen-year-old Georgiana, marriage meant freedom and an entrance into the great world. An observer at a court function wrote:

> The Drawing Room was fuller than I ever saw it excepting of a birthday, owing, I suppose, to the curiosity to see the Duchess of Devonshire. She looked very pretty and happiness was never more marked in a countenance than in hers. She was properly fine for the time of year, and her diamonds are very magnificent: the girdle is a piece of finery so uncommon it made it all the more admired. The Duke of Devonshire had very near been too late: it was nearly four o'clock when he came in to the Drawing Room. I make no doubt but His Grace is as happy as his duchess, but his countenance does not mark it so strongly.

Indeed, very little emotion was ever seen on the Duke's face. He was altogether a strange man, taciturn and cold. In looks he was handsome and well built, in mind intelligent and cultivated, with a reputation for classical scholarship. Yet he seemed to care for little except women and cards. The heir to high political position, he spoke only twice in the House of Lords and never played a significant role in government. Perhaps everything had come to him too easily. Some years later, a great Whig hostess asked her guests what the wretchedest kind of man could be. People made the obvious guesses, but gave her the prize when she concluded that it was a handsome duke. A man who is born with looks, intelligence, wealth, and power is left with no challenge; all prizes lose their value.

The handsome Duke of Devonshire, however, appreciated his wife's success and helped her to create the most important salon in London. Within a year the Duchess was the undisputed queen of the Whigs. Along with the prominent nobles, she received Fox, Burke, Sheridan, Walpole, Gibbon, Dr. Johnson, Reynolds, Gainsborough, and all the prettiest women in London. Soon there was no fashion except that found at Devonshire House, and the Duke went back to his cards and his mistresses.

Obviously the Duchess's money and position were attractions, but beyond these, Georgiana had a kind of fascination that made people want to know her. "The Duchess of Devonshire effaces all without being a beauty," Walpole wrote in 1775, "but her youth, figure, flowing good nature, sense, and lively modesty and modest familiarity make her a phenomenon." Although she was good-looking, it was evidently her charm, her warmth, her disregard for the conventional that made almost everyone love her. She had, said a woman-about-town, "kindness embellished by politeness," and a society writer added that she was not really very beautiful but "possessed an ardent temper, susceptible of deep as well as strong impressions; a cultivated understanding, illuminated by a taste for poetry and the fine arts; much sensibility not exempt, perhaps, from vanity and coquetry."

That first summer of her marriage, the Duchess spent several weeks at Chatsworth, the grand country palace built by an earlier duke. There she took music and painting lessons, played the harpsichord, and read a great deal—particularly history, the better to understand her own time. There too, in those sumptuous rooms, all the Whig leaders came to talk to her. Of course they were against the American war—less, perhaps, from love of liberty than because it was the King's war, and Lord North, the Prime Minister, could be thrown out of office if only he lost to the rebels. Politics were beginning to dominate English conversation. "I wish there were any other topic of discourse than politics," Walpole wrote a little later, "but one can hear, one can talk nor think on anything else. It has pervaded all ranks and ages. A miss, not fourteen, asked Miss Agnes Berry, lately, whether she was an aristocrat or a democrat."

The Duchess would have had no hesitation in answering that question: she was already an enthusiastic democrat. The term was relative, of course. Both Chatsworth and Devonshire House were palaces filled with gilded furniture and staffed by dozens of servants. Lady Caroline Lamb, the

Duchess's niece, who was educated at Devonshire House, once revealed what she considered to be extreme poverty: "Would you believe," she said, "that the unfortunate lady didn't even have a Groom of the Chamber?"

Certainly the Duchess was not about to lack for anything, and as soon as she returned to London, she launched into a gay life where fashion was the main concern. Across the Channel another young woman, Marie Antoinette, felt the same passion for clothes, and soon Georgiana was importing the extravagant styles first worn by the French Queen. To the horror of dowdy, plain Queen Charlotte, the Duchess's hooped skirts became larger and larger until they were as much as fourteen feet around. Then her coiffures began reaching higher and higher. These towers of powdered hair were adorned with huge bunches of plumes, the Duchess's triumph coming on the day when she found an ostrich feather four feet long. The Queen let it be known that she would have no feathers at court, but no one cared. Georgiana was too grand to be ignored, even by royalty, and soon anyone with any pretensions to fashion was imitating the lively Duchess.

The Duchess seemed mad for pleasure. There were balls—for she loved to dance—and country fetes, the opera, and the theater. At Devonshire House she gave famous late-night suppers for the most brilliant men, the prettiest women in London. Those who were invited rushed to attend; the others, consumed with jealousy, muttered darkly about orgies.

London wasn't Versailles, though; when the season ended early in August, everyone went back to the country, where the pace was less frantic. People visited, of course—even the solemn Dr. Johnson, one of the Duchess's favorites, came to see her. Georgiana wrote her mother: "He din'd here and does not shine quite so much in eating as in conversing, for he eats much and nastily." Walpole, never one to ignore a fashionable duchess, also came often. Of course, the conversation often turned to politics, the American insurgents, and their Declaration of Independence; but even that burning topic did not prevent Georgiana from spending much time alone on her great avocation, writing. At first she composed poetry, as in these lines of 1775 about parting:

> No Rose could ever droop its head
> As Summers much loved moments fled
> Could ne'er its grief sincere impart
> In sign of melancholy woe
> With half the grief that feels my heart
> When what it loves is forced to go. . . .

The form is perhaps a little stilted, the imagery slightly shopworn, but there is a genuine lyric quality to the work. And for a young, pretty, and fashionable duchess, the melancholy seems curiously genuine.

When Marie Antoinette and Georgiana met during one of the Devonshires' frequent trips abroad in the eighties, they liked each other instantly. Except for the Duchess's greater intelligence, in fact, they were not unalike. Particularly when they were both very young (in 1780 the Duchess was twenty-three, the Queen twenty-four) and unhappily married, they behaved in very similar ways. They found amusement in ceaseless entertainment and crowds of followers. Even their sex lives were not dissimilar: neither was really her husband's wife. Legend notwithstanding, however, Marie Antoinette remained faithful with one possible exception, while Georgiana soon found falling in and out of love the most thrilling of occupations. Unlike her French contemporaries, she never slept with a man unless she was really in love with him. It was just that she often felt disappointed by men whose qualities turned out to be illusions.

Still, Georgiana surrounded herself with far more interesting people than Marie Antoinette did. In 1776 she visited the House of Commons for the first time and heard Charles Fox speak, and by 1777 he was one of the stars of her salon. She wrote her mother: "I have always thought that the greatest merit of C. Fox is his amazing quickness in seizing any subject—he seems to have the particular talent of knowing more about what he is saying and with less pains than anybody else—his conversation is like a brilliant player at billiards, the strokes follow one another, piff-paff."

The grandson of the Duke of Richmond and the son of Lord Holland, Fox was connected with all the great Whig families. Both his position in society and his remarkable ability were elements in a highly successful career. This wonderfully sharp and eloquent man also managed to make himself loved, not only by his many mistresses but by his friends as well. He had started out as a macaroni, or fop—that English equivalent of the French *agréable*—but soon lost interest in clothes and fashion. He drank a great deal, but so did everyone else, including his dear friend the Prince of Wales. The Prince needed no encouragement

in dissipation, but the King, horrified by his son's loose living, chose to blame Fox for leading the young man astray. Then too, Fox gambled maniacally. Although he was very good at cards and often won, he managed to lose all his other bets, so that he was soon not just penniless but heavily in debt.

"Charles is unquestionably a man of first-rate talents," his best friend wrote, "but so deficient in judgment as never to have succeeded in any object during his whole life. He loved only three things—women, play, and politics. Yet at no period did he ever form a creditable connection with a woman. He lost his whole fortune at the gaming table; and with the exception of about eleven months of his life, he has remained always in opposition." As for the last, it was no wonder. George III, a notoriously vindictive man, nurtured a passionate hatred for Fox because he was brilliant and disrespectful, because he made fun of the King in public, and because he provided a center for the Prince of Wales's group of anti-Crown opponents.

The other great man at Devonshire House was Richard Sheridan, the playwright. Although he had no high family connections like Fox, this son of an actor was so witty, so amusing, yet so lacking in malice that he became indispensable to Georgiana and her friends. *The School for Scandal* owes much to what the author could see in the Duchess's salon.

The tone at Devonshire House was unquestionably sophisticated, yet very different from that of a French salon. It was a little less witty, perhaps, and less formal. Certainly it was enormously more romantic: the main characteristic of that circle, from the Prince of Wales on down, was that all were governed by their feelings. It was a society where rules need not even be broken since they were completely ignored; where the outside world exacted no compliance; where money, although almost everyone had enormous debts, never seemed to be a problem. There was nothing to do, really, but pay attention to your emotions; and this morbid concentration on every fugitive sensation often caused great unhappiness.

Although the Duchess herself was relatively restrained, most members of the Devonshire House circle were really quite dissolute. The Prince of Wales consumed both wine and women in quantity. Then in the 1780s he secretly married an actress, to whom he was soon unfaithful. Fox slept with every woman he could. The Duke of Devonshire always had a mistress and was the father of a number of bastards. Georgiana's sister Lady Bessborough was given to dramatic, if sometimes brief, affairs, a tendency inherited by her daughter, the famous Lady Caroline Lamb.

In 1780 the Duchess inaugurated a new *ménage à trois* by providing her husband with a mistress right in Devonshire House. Lady Elizabeth Foster, the daughter of the Earl of Bristol, was a young woman of exceptional charm, intelligence, and education. She had just left her husband and was consequently in need of earning her living. Meanwhile at Devonshire House there was an illegitimate daughter of the Duke's who needed looking after. The solution was obvious: Lady Elizabeth became the child's titular governess. It all worked out very nicely; the child was, naturally, never seen downstairs, and Lady Elizabeth became one of the stars of Georgiana's salon. In short order the two women were best friends and spent hours every day exchanging confidences.

Conveniently, the Duke also liked the new governess, so with the full agreement of the Duchess, Lady Elizabeth kept him happy. Whenever she became pregnant, Georgiana was kindness itself. The children were brought up at Devonshire House, and the threesome lived happily ever after.

The Duchess liked to gamble, mostly at cards, and she played for enormous stakes. No wonder, really: in a life where everything was so safe, so well established, so ultimately unsatisfying, only gambling whipped up excitement. Her losses accumulated, however, and in 1782 Georgiana reached an impasse: she owed the huge sum of £150,000 and could not pay it. She went to her family, but they couldn't—or wouldn't—supply the money. Instead they advised her to ask the Duke; they even offered to conduct the negotiations. When approached, the Duke listened politely. He was willing, he said, to pay off his wife's debts, but he needed an heir. If Georgiana would agree to sleep with him, he would take care of the money.

At first the Duchess was horrified. She had made it very plain before the wedding that she didn't love the Duke and wouldn't allow the marriage to be consummated. He had agreed at the time, but now he wanted an heir to his title and fortune. Under a good deal of pressure from the Spencers, Georgiana finally capitulated. In 1783 her first child was born; unfortunately for the Duke, it was a daughter.

The next time Georgiana's debts became unmanageable, she consented once again to share her husband's bed. Another daughter was born. At last, in 1790, she produced a son. The three-cornered relationship continued all the while; just because she had given in three times, Georgiana saw no reason to make it a habit. So Lady Elizabeth kept the Duke contented while remaining the Duchess's best friend. As for the offspring, Georgiana, who had been much impressed by Rousseau's *Emile*, turned out to be a model mother. Unlike just about anyone else in England, she concerned herself with her children, took care of them, and actually made them happy.

Having children was all very well, but with brief exceptions, it was hardly time-consuming. Just then, because of the American insurgency, English politics were livelier than usual. Soon the Duchess became personally involved. The subject, after all, was part of her inheritance: the Whigs were born to rule England. Now, however, the King had stopped being a cipher and was trying to rule it himself. Since the Whigs believed in a kind of aristocratic republic in which the Crown was virtually powerless, he set to securing Tory majorities. Although it helped him eventually to have the Tory leader William Pitt on his side, it wasn't essential. In a pinch a lapsed Whig like Lord North would do just as well; and since the Commons were used to being bought, the buying would now be done by the King. Obviously, the Devonshires found this new trend deplorable. When elections were called in 1784, it became evident not only that George III was intent on securing a Tory majority, but that he planned to keep Fox out of Parliament as well.

In the eighteenth century, elections were spread over several weeks. Voters in a constituency often had as much as two months to walk in and proclaim their preference (the secret ballot had not yet been invented). In Fox's case, the voters of Westminster could make their opinion known at any time between April 1 and May 17. And during those six weeks, George III showed plainly that he considered results in Westminster to be of major importance. Fox, the King thought, was responsible for the Prince of Wales's hostility. In fact, the Prince was simply following the tradition

Rowlandson. *The Devonshire*. One in a series of cartoons mocking the Duchess of Devonshire's electioneering. Print Collection, Art, Prints and Photographs Division, The New York Public Library, Astor, Lenox and Tilden Foundations

in which the heir to the throne was also the leader of the opposition, and Fox was helping him behave according to custom. Then too, Fox had held office in a previous government and had sponsored an anti-corruption bill that would have freed several M.P.s from the Crown's influence. It was not to be borne.

Westminster was a two-member constituency, and in 1784 three candidates were fighting for the two seats. One was a gallant and victorious admiral who was sure to be elected. The question became which of the others, Fox or Sir Cecil Wray, would run second. The King was so passionately involved in Wray's candidacy that Dr. Johnson said, "Only think, Sir, it was a struggle between George the Third's scepter and Mr. Fox's tongue." The Duchess of Devonshire, of course, was ready to fight for Fox.

The result was one of the most corrupt elections in English politics. Naturally both sides supplied the electors with free beer. Wray imported a group of sailors to beat up voters who declared for Fox. In retaliation Fox brought in a crowd of hackney coachmen who beat up the sailors, and the streets became unsafe. The King let it be known that all loyal subjects were expected to vote for Wray. The Prince of Wales came out in favor of Fox, "the man of the people," and, wearing *true blue*, the colors of the American insurgents, he took to spending his afternoons at Devonshire House planning what to do next.

The opposition spoke of Fox as a dissolute, drunken gambler. Fox claimed that Wray wanted to levy a tax on servant girls that would reduce them to prostitution, since they would become too expensive to hire as domestics. Wray bribed the voters; Fox bought them back through an ingenious device.

Fox's agent would walk up to an elector and say, "I'll wager five guineas that you will not vote for Fox."

"Done!" the man would reply, cast his vote for Fox, and pocket the five guineas.

As the days passed, however, it became clear that Fox was losing. The Duchess began to drive her own gig from house to house asking for votes. In later years one of the Westminster voters described it:

> Lord, Sir, it was a fine sight to see a grand lady come right smack to us hard-working mortals, with a hand held out and a "Master, how-dye-do," and a laugh so loud, and a talk so kind, and shake us by the hand and say "Give us your vote, worthy sir, a plumper for the people's friend, our friend, everybody's friend!" . . . and then, sir, they'd think nothing of a kiss, aye, a dozen of them.

It was shocking: a Duchess walking the streets and kissing workingmen! And since this particular duchess was so charming, it was effective enough to make the Tories take fright. It was time, they decided, to fight fire with fire, so they sent out the good-looking Marchioness of Salisbury, lips at the ready:

> She canvass'd all, both great and small,
> And thunder'd at each door, Sir;
> She rummag'd every shop and stall—
> The Duchess had been before her.

The Duchess, in fact, had even gone so far as to kiss a butcher; and she brought in Fox. When the votes were counted, Admiral Hood led with 6,694; Fox followed (and was elected) with 6,233; Wray was out with 5,998. It was a triumph for the Duchess, the Prince of Wales, and the Whigs; the court could scarcely hide its fury. Not only had Georgiana beaten the King; she had also been given what she always said was her favorite compliment: "Your eyes are so bright, my Lady," a laborer told her, "that I could light my pipe at them."

Except at the height of the Westminster contest, the Duchess's social life went on, busy as ever. There were concerts and masquerades, balls and water fetes at the Devonshire villa near Chiswick. After the American war had ended, the French discovered they were Anglophiles; going to London suddenly became chic. Led by the duc d'Orléans, the King's cousin, the French aristocracy streamed across the Channel and added to the gaiety of the London season. Even in 1789, when the visitors became emigrés, the festivities continued. The French assumed that they would soon be going home; the Whigs assumed that the Revolution would lead to a parliamentary monarchy;

everyone was tactful and went right on having fun.

Even then Georgiana wrote, and wrote, and wrote. Sometimes it was a novel like *The Sylph,* a story in epistolary form about a debauched husband (who commits suicide in the end) and an ever more virtuous wife (who ends well). On the whole, this book—pseudonymous, since it would never do for a duchess to write a novel—is pretty dull. There are a few entertaining descriptions of fashionable life, but the characters are shallow, the action predictable, and the style often awkward.

It was for her verse that the Duchess became known, since she could claim authorship because poetry was considered a nobler genre. In 1793 she published her *Passage of the Mountain of Saint Gothard* to universal acclaim. It was translated into French, German, and Italian, and the Duchess found herself firmly ensconced in the literary pantheon. Taste has changed, and to the modern eye her verse often seems awkward and artificial:

> And hail the chapel! Hail the platform wild
> Where Tell directed the avenging dart
> With well strung arm that first preserved the child,
> Then winged the arrow to the tyrant's heart,
> Where three Swiss heroes lawless force withstood
> And stamped the freedom of their native land.

Unfortunately, when the meter becomes sprightlier, in the Duchess's *Lines on the Battle of Aboukir,* the subject is inappropriately grim:

> I am wretched, past retrieving;
> He is lost and I'm undone
> All my life will pass in grieving
> For the battle we have won.

Somehow, the tears don't flow.

As the nineties came around, the Duchess was apparently unchanged, apparently still young. Fanny Burney met her at Bath in 1791, and like the rest of the world, was entranced:

> I do not find so much beauty in her as I expected, notwithstanding the variation of accounts; but I found in her more of manner, politeness, and gentle quiet. She seems by nature to possess the highest animal spirits, but she appeared to me not happy. I thought she looked oppressed within, though there

is a native cheerfulness about her which I fancy scarce deserts her.

> There is in her face, especially when she speaks, a sweetness of good humor and obligingness that seem to be natural and instinctive qualities of her disposition; joined to an openness of countenance that announces her endowed by nature with a character intended wholly for honesty, fairness, and good purpose.

The words "nature" and "natural" come up remarkably often in descriptions of Georgiana. It was most unusual to find a grande dame who was so absolutely herself.

Three days later the Duchess seemed a little more cheerful. Miss Burney met her again and wrote:

> I now saw the Duchess far more easy and lively in her spirits and, consequently, far more lovely in her person. Vivacity is so much her characteristic that her style of beauty requires it indispensably; the beauty, indeed, dies away without it. I now saw how her fame for personal charms had been obtained; the expression of her style is so very sweet, and has an ingenuousness and openness so singular that, taken in those moments, not the most rigid critic could deny the justice of her personal celebrity. She was quite gay, easy, and charming; indeed, that last epithet might have been coined for her.

A few years earlier, the loveliness would have been more constant: the Duchess was beginning to weary. All through the nineties, as Europe was devoured by revolution and war, England, safe behind its navy, went on living as if nothing had happened. Devonshire House, Chatsworth, Chiswick opened their doors to gay, ornate throngs. The Duchess still gave fashionable parties; the Prince of Wales still came for dinner and got drunk. Even in England, however, it became obvious that the world had changed. The executions of Louis XVI and Marie Antoinette shocked everyone. Even the Whigs turned anti-French, and the Tories, as the party most fiercely opposed to the Revolution, were firmly in power.

All the fun at Devonshire House began to take on a mechanical quality. The Duchess gambled more than ever and for ever higher stakes, but after his son was born, the Duke no longer

paid up. Bailiffs stood at the door of Devonshire House, and Georgiana had to leap into her carriage so as not to be seized by them. There was a brief flurry of excitement in her circle when Fox joined the Grenville government on Pitt's death. Almost immediately, however, Fox too was dead. Nothing really mattered anymore.

Perhaps the Duchess had led too self-indulgent a life; every pleasure must eventually pall. Perhaps she belonged too much to the eighteenth century to enjoy the new spirit of 1789. In any event, her last years had a ghostly quality: life went on as before, but without substance. In 1796 the Duchess lost most of the sight in one eye; flesh and blood were becoming shadow.

Little by little the Duchess became duller, less fashionable. Younger hostesses sprang up, so that the habitués of Devonshire House dwindled to a small, dreadfully bored circle. When other people dropped in occasionally, they could hardly believe that the fading belle who rattled on and on had once been so lively, so amusing. In March, 1806, the Duchess fell ill. One cannot help suspecting she was glad; and quickly, easily, before the month was out, she was dead.

Mme Vigée-Lebrun. *Rose Bertin.*
Photograph courtesy of the
Frick Art Reference Library, New York

Working Women
Rose Bertin
Madame Vigée-Lebrun

Besides politics, Mrs. Adams and the Duchess of Devonshire shared another interest: they both loved hats. (Mrs. Adams's first move when she arrived in Paris was to go out and buy a fashionable bonnet.) In fact, both briefly patronized the same *modiste*—although that was hardly surprising, for if you really wanted to be fashionable, if you were trying to buy the very best, then only the great Mademoiselle Bertin would do.

There had been other successful dress and hat designers, but each had a limited clientele and achieved no particular fame. Then in 1773 Mlle Bertin opened her shop, and within a year her creations were admired all over Europe. She might charge more, or treat customers rudely, or make herself inaccessible, but at a time when fashion was all, it was Mlle Bertin who created fashion. In doing so, she founded the very first of the *haute couture* houses.

Rose Bertin—her real, less glamorous name was Marie Jeanne—was born in 1747 to a respectable lower-class family in northern France. Her father and uncles were bricklayers and carpenters, her mother a housewife. They must have needed money: at the age of nine the little girl was apprenticed to Mme Barbier, a dressmaker in Abbeville. The child obviously pleased her employer, because she stayed for a full fourteen years. Then in 1770 she moved to Paris and, provincial that she was, opened a shop on the unfashionable Quai de Gesvres. She quickly saw her mistake: within three years she had established herself on the chic, luxurious rue Saint Honoré.

That this dumpy little woman with a pert, turned-up nose had a flair for fashion was obvious. Within a year of her arrival in Paris, she was already selling to that epitome of elegance, Mme du Barry. It was only in 1774, though, that she found her greatest client. At first the Dauphine—who spent far too much time with those sour spinsters, Mesdames Adélaide and Victoire (the daughters of Louis XV and the aunts of Louis

Cochin. *The Ladies' Tailor.* The Metropolitan Museum of Art, New York. The Elisha Whittelsey Collection, The Elisha Whittelsey Fund, 1949 (49.50.242)

XVI)—had been distinctly dowdy. Her mother, the empress Maria Theresa, who was always ready with a reprimand, wrote telling her to pay more attention to her clothes. "It is up to you to set the tone at Versailles," she chided. When the Dauphine became Queen after Louis XV's death and was staying at Marly, the duchesse de Chartres presented Rose Bertin to her. Like a dutiful daughter, the new sovereign remembered her mother's instructions and paid attention to the dressmaker.

Suddenly Marie Antoinette, who was eighteen then, understood how much fun it could be to lead the fashion. She began conferring with Mlle Bertin about the shape of hats and the decor of dresses. Soon the couturiere was coming to Versailles twice a week to "work with Her Majesty," and the sovereign made it known that her ambition was to be not a great queen, but the most fashionable woman in the kingdom.

The current styles lent themselves particularly well to Mlle Bertin's talent. The oblong hooped skirts, in fashion since the 1720s, had recently begun to swell until they often reached over six feet from right to left, and that vast acreage of fabric cried out for decoration. Because of guild regulations, Mlle Bertin never made a dress herself. She chose the material, decided on the width of the pannier, and sent her order to a tailor, who stitched up the unadorned garment. Then the real work started. Both bodice and skirt were decorated with an endless array of draped fabric, embroidery, lace, flowers, spangles, tassels, and sometimes precious stones. No two dresses were ever alike, and only Mlle Bertin understood how to give them exactly the right look.

Here, for instance, is a court presentation dress made for Mme de Chatenay in 1786. First, 99 ells (an estimated 33 yards) of black velvet were ordered for the skirt, bodice, and train. Then the skirt was garnished at the bottom with a small flounce of black gauze. The flounce was trimmed with an embroidered gauze made to look like lace and surmounted with a wide velvet appliqué embroidered with precious stones and spangles in the form of a chain. The bottom embroidery was shaped like a fringe and ended in a true fringe of silver tassels and crystal beads. On the right and left of the skirt, a black velvet drapery was embroidered on the bias with precious stones and spangles. Its border was a tasseled fringe of very rich crystal beads. The back and train of the skirt were decorated with a black leaf garland held in place by folded, cut-out black satin. The bodice was adorned with a wide embroidery, all in precious stones, as were the shoulder pieces. Five velvet bows embroidered with precious stones were attached to the train. The sleeves were of striped gauze. This ensemble was worn with two bracelets made of black gauze and shirred black velvet; a necklace of velvet embroidered with precious stones; and at the side of the bodice, a fine bouquet of white lilacs and roses. The price was 1,235 livres—just under $4,000.

To our modern eye the figure seems reason-able, but in the 1770s and 1780s there were constant complaints that Mlle Bertin's bills were ruinous. Of course, they could mount up. Marie Antoinette spent 258,352 livres (approximately $700,000) on clothes in 1785, a year in which she had supposedly lost all interest in fashion. Only 91,947 livres ($275,000) of the total went to Mlle Bertin, whose success had by that time attracted rivals. For comparison, note that the Queen's official dress budget was only 120,000 livres and that 50,000 livres was considered a large yearly income. A very rich duchess thought herself fortunate if her entire income was close to what the Queen spent on her dresses.

There were many women who could not afford court presentation gowns but went to Mlle Bertin for her remarkable hats. It was even fashionable for men to give ladies Bertin hats as presents. If you wanted to go all out, you would have paid 120 livres ($360) in 1777 for a hat with a fine-pleated lace border, a tulle veil, a crown of Italian gauze and white satin with a black velvet stripe, garnishes of rosebud branches, and a panache of white feathers. For 240 livres ($720) you could have bought that expensive rarity, a fine heron feather, which Léonard, the fashionable hairdresser, would use in your coiffure. Or if these prices were beyond your means, for 54 livres ($162) you could have bought a yellow straw hat lined in taffeta, garlanded with poppies, tulips, cornflowers, and wheat ears, and trimmed at the back with a white feather.

Just because Rose Bertin was successful didn't mean she was loved. The middle classes accused her of ruining France by encouraging the Queen's extravagance; the upper classes found her uppity. The baronne d'Oberkirch, an Alsatian lady who came to Paris now and again, describes her experience with the great couturiere:

On May 28 [1784], I still hadn't visited Mlle Bertin but everyone had been telling me about the wonders she had wrought. She was more fashionable than ever and people fought over her hats. She showed me several, that day, *herself,* which was no mean privilege, at least thirty altogether, and each different from the others. . . . I owed the *kindness* of Mlle Bertin to my friendship with Madame la com-

Hats similar to those produced by Mlle Bertin, a plate from
Le Cabinet des Modes. The Metropolitan Museum of Art,
New York. Harris Brisbane Dick Fund, 1938 (38.38.6)

tesse du Nord [the wife of the tsarevich Paul] who
was still one of her clients. This little chit's jargon
was most entertaining; it was a mixture of pride
and obsequiousness which came close to impertinence unless one took care to keep her down.

One cannot help wondering whether the
baroness wasn't bragging a little. It would have
taken a bold woman indeed to keep Mlle Bertin
down—especially since "there was a little Bohemian hat, its brim curled up with a rare perfection, made from a model given by a lady of that
country, and about which everyone in Paris was
absolutely mad."

Mme d'Oberkirch was not the only one to
complain about Mlle Bertin's arrogance. The *Correspondance secrète,* a gossip and information sheet,
related in April, 1778, what happened to ladies
who weren't lucky enough to be friends of the
wife of the tsarevich:

A noble lady came to ask Mlle Bertin for several
hats she wanted to take back to her province. The
dressmaker, lying down on her chaise longue and
wearing an elegant negligee, scarcely bothered to
acknowledge the noble lady, only nodding to her
[instead of curtsying]. She rings. A charming young
nymph called Mlle Adélaide appears. "Show Madame last month's hats," says Mlle Bertin. The lady
says she would like to see some newer ones. "That
isn't possible, Madame," the dressmaker answers,
"the very last time I worked with the Queen, we
decided that the newest hats would not be shown
for another week." Ever since then Mlle Bertin has
been called the minister of fashion.

For the times, this behavior was shocking. A
working woman simply did not treat a provincial
noble lady as an equal. It demonstrated that Mlle
Bertin was conscious of the magnitude of her talent; some vanity may have been mixed with her
pretensions, but she also knew what she was
worth. And as far as we can determine, she was
sufficiently devoted to her calling to have had neither husband nor lover. Apparently couture was
everything to her.

As horrifying as her impertinence, many
people thought, was Mlle Bertin's direct contact
with the Queen. Until then the queens of France
had never ordered their clothes directly, much

Ballgown (robe à la française), French.
The Metropolitan Museum of Art, New York.
Gift of Fédération de la Soierie, 1950
(CI 50.168.2ab)

Fan. Paper and ivory.
The Metropolitan Museum of Art, New York.
Bequest of Mary Strong Shattuck, 1935 (35.80.12)

Fan. Paper and ivory. The Metropolitan Museum of Art, New York.
Gift of Mrs. William Randolph Hearst, 1963 (63.90.53)

less conferred with a dressmaker. Their *dame
d'atours* (Mistress of the Robes) did the ordering
for them, and in consequence they often looked
dowdy, if sumptuous. Now, to her horror, the
dame d'atours found herself frozen out. The Queen's
ladies-in-waiting, whose privilege it was to attend
her, were left behind in the state bedroom as
Marie Antoinette retired to her private apartments
with Rose Bertin. As a result, of course, everybody was outraged. Even the adoring Mme Campan, the Queen's Woman of the Bedchamber,
looked at Mlle Bertin with envy and disapproval.

She wrote:

> It is fair to say that the admission of a dressmaker
> into the Queen's apartments had unfortunate results
> for Her Majesty. The skill of the shopkeeper, re-
> ceived in private despite the custom which kept out
> all people of her class, without exception, made it
> easier for her to advocate a new fashion every day.
>
> Every lady immediately wanted to have the
> same adornments as the Queen, to wear those
> plumes, those garlands to which her beauty, which
> was then at its height, gave an infinite charm. All
> the younger ladies' bills immediately went up; the
> mothers and the husbands complained, a few care-
> less women went into debt, there were family
> scenes, several couples found their relationship cool-
> ing or even broken off, and gossip had it that the
> Queen would be the ruin of all French ladies.

Soon Mlle Bertin was conferring with the
Queen so long and so frequently that she was
forced to rent an apartment near the palace in
Versailles. As for Marie Antoinette, she gained a
reputation for extreme and incurable frivolity
which was not altogether undeserved. Maria Theresa, of course, was the first to complain. When
her daughter sent her a portrait in which she was
shown wearing her new finery, together with a
letter saying that she had obeyed her mother's orders to dress up, the Empress replied: "This was
not the portrait of a Queen of France, but of
an actress. . . . You know that I think fashion
should be followed moderately, but never to any
extreme. A young and pretty Queen, attractive in
herself, has no need for these follies."

Marie Antoinette disagreed; the conferences
with Mlle Bertin continued. The two women
poured over samples—of fabric, embroidery,
feathers, flowers—and decided each week just
what the fashion would be the next.

In 1779 when the Queen gave birth to her
first child and announced that henceforth she
would pay less attention to fashion, she still invited Mlle Bertin to the court's private theater at
Marly. More amazingly, when Marie Antoinette
came to Paris to celebrate the birth of the baby,
and her carriage passed in front of Mlle Bertin's
shop, Her Majesty was seen to nod, smile, and
wave to the ecstatic couturiere curtsying madly

Moreau le Jeune. *The Queen's Lady in Waiting.* A fine example
of the sort of dress produced by Mlle Bertin in collaboration
with Marie Antoinette. The Metropolitan Museum of Art,
New York. Harris Brisbane Dick Fund, 1933 (33.6.3)

Angelica Kauffmann. *Maria Carolina of Naples with Her Husband and Children*. Queen Maria Carolina, who was Marie Antoinette's sister and ruled over Naples (see Chapter 7), was a client of Mlle Bertin. Collection of the ruling princes of Liechtenstein, Vaduz

on her balcony. When Louis XVI followed suit, so did every courtier in the long train of carriages.

No one who visited her shop could have doubted that Mlle Bertin was firmly established. On the outside, wide windows framed in panels of simulated lavender and yellow marble beckoned you in. After you had crossed a room occupied by two bookkeepers, you entered the main part of the shop. This was decorated with portraits of the Queens of France, Sweden, Spain, Portugal, and Naples, as well as the Empress of Russia—all clients of Mlle Bertin. There the new fashions were displayed. Sometimes they spread into the next room too—as on the occasion when 280 dresses worth half a million livres were shown to the public before being sent on to Madrid. Crowds naturally flocked to see them, and Mlle Bertin, who knew her own worth, once answered a client who complained that the prices were too high: "What, Monsieur! Would you pay a great artist no more than the cost of his canvas and paints?" In fact her prices were not quite what they seemed since many nobles who were spending above their means simply ignored their bills when they ran out of cash. In one spectacular case, that of the prince de Guéménée, the result was bankruptcy. By the time the prince realized in 1783 that he had been a little careless, he owed six million livres ($18 million), and Mlle Bertin, like many other tradespeople, felt the pinch. The Guéménées were by no means alone. While it is difficult to arrive at an exact figure, probably no more than half of her bills were paid within a year of their receipt, and about 20 percent were never paid at all.

While Mlle Bertin's clients neglected to pay her, she had to provide wages for thirty seamstresses working above the shop and meet bills for the lavish materials of her trade—fabrics, feathers, spangles, gold and silver thread, silk flowers, lace. As a result, this phenomenally successful couturiere always had money problems; in 1783, in fact, she was forced to move to a cheaper location.

This is not to say that she was poor. In 1782 she bought herself a large house standing in a sizable garden at Epinay-sur-Seine near Paris. Just before the Revolution, she also acquired a small

apartment building in Paris. She was never rich, however, and when the courtiers started emigrating, her situation grew worse. Not only did their bills remain unpaid, but by 1791 no one thought of buying clothes anymore—no one, that is, except Marie Antoinette.

The Queen went on ordering clothes until the very end. When she and Louis XVI fled from Paris, they took along several heavy trunks full of court costumes. The weight of all this luggage slowed down their carriage and was partly responsible for their being caught at Varennes. Even after their dreadful trip back to Paris, during which Marie Antoinette's hair turned white overnight, she continued to order court dresses. For example, there was a brown silk one, richly adorned with lace and embroidered in white satin, which she wore on All Hallows' Eve, 1791. To be fair, it must be said that her dress bill declined by half that year: it was only a little over 44,000 livres ($132,000). Even in 1792 after the royal family was imprisoned in the Temple, orders still went to Mlle Bertin and clothes came from her shop. The bills, however, were addressed to the · government of the French Republic.

By then it was no longer the couturiere herself who filled the orders. In July, 1792, she set off for Koblenz, where a number of her clients had taken refuge. She was far too shrewd to emigrate and thus forfeit all her possessions in France. Instead, she went to the authorities and explained that since no one was buying her clothes in Paris and she herself had debts, she needed to take her stock abroad and liquidate it there. A passport was granted, and she went off to provide all those poor, dowdy foreigners with fashionable clothes. Cleverly, she kept sending small sums back to France to keep her status. After a while, however, it occurred to the revolutionary government that the woman who had benefited from Marie Antoinette's profligacy really ought to be tried and beheaded, or, if she was unavailable, she should at least be added to the list of emigrés.

As soon as Mlle Bertin heard the news, she wrote back indignantly while prudently staying out of reach. At the end of January, 1795, she was crossed off the list. Still, she decided against

taking any risks and didn't return until 1800, when things had settled down nicely and Bonaparte had restored order. She had no reason to hurry back in any case: she had been doing well abroad and came home a good deal richer. Among other ventures, she had run a successful money-lending business.

By 1800 fashion was very different from what it had been in the last years of the ancien régime. Josephine Bonaparte, the new trend setter, had her own favorite, Leroy. There was really no room for Mlle Bertin, so she passed her shop on to her nephew, retired, and moved to her house in Epinay. She died there in 1813, quite forgotten by everyone in Paris. After the Bourbons came back in 1814, however, one of the first people for whom the restored Louis XVIII asked was Mlle Bertin, perhaps for memory's sake, perhaps because his niece, the duchesse d'Angoulême, wanted to bring back the fashions of her childhood. When he was told that the couturiere had died a year earlier, he expressed great regret. It seems a fitting epitaph for Marie Antoinette's minister of fashion that a proper court had become almost unimaginable without the genius of Mlle Bertin.

Mme Vigée-Lebrun. *Marie Antoinette*. The Queen's
portrait is the work of her favorite painter, a
woman whose career dazzled her contemporaries.
Kunsthistorisches Museum, Vienna

Mme Vigée-Lebrun. *Self-Portrait*.
This is the portrait that launched
the artist's career in Rome.
Scala/Editorial Photocolor Archives,
Inc., New York

Madame Vigée-Lebrun

Madame Vigée-Lebrun, Marie Antoinette's favorite painter, was luckier than Rose Bertin in that she lived long enough to see the monarchy restored. Like Mlle Bertin, she showed that it was possible for a working woman of no birth at all to achieve fame and fortune; but while she too was a client of the great dressmaker, Mme Vigée-Lebrun considered herself vastly superior to Rose Bertin both socially and intellectually. After all, she had become a hugely successful artist by the time she was twenty-five. She was invited everywhere, and the greatest names in France attended her parties. When she traveled abroad, her hostesses and clients everywhere belonged to the most exalted circles.

Elisabeth Louise Vigée, the daughter of a third-rate painter, was born in April, 1755. Her talent showed early, so M. Vigée set her to copying the masters and saw to it that she received advice from Vernet and Greuze. Since Diderot, d'Alembert, and Helvétius were friends of the family, the young girl was also introduced early to the art of conversation.

When she was thirteen, her father died. Her mother soon remarried, and the new stepfather turned out to be nasty and mean. Clearly there was only one way out: Elisabeth Louise started painting portraits of all the people around her. Soon she was producing charming likenesses, and word of her talent began to spread. By 1774, when she was barely nineteen, her work was selling, her fame was growing—and every penny she made went straight into the stepfather's pocket. Still, her life had its pleasures. She had begun to meet glamorous people, and there was always the excitement of the city.

The world of Paris before the Revolution had infinite charms that Mme Vigée-Lebrun never ceased regretting. She talks longingly in her memoirs about the elegant Thursdays on the boulevard du Temple, with its rows of carriages pulled by beautifully matched horses; about the puppet shows; about the rouged old ladies sitting and gossiping about twenty-year-old scandals. She speaks of the naumachias, those carefully set "naval battles" in the great rotunda of the Champs-Elysées. She describes the elegant crowds that came out of the Opéra into the gardens of the Palais Royal at two in the morning, the women in their huge, sumptuous gowns, their hair dressed with perfumed powder, their bosoms adorned with bouquets of rare and splendid flowers. It was a world of pleasure, sophistication, and luxury, a world in which, she tells us, "beauty could really make you famous." Young Mlle Vigée, need one say it, was uncommonly pretty.

It was in those Palais Royal gardens, on which her windows opened, that the young painter met the duchesse de Chartres, a princess of the blood royal and her first illustrious client. In the same year the duchesse introduced Mlle Bertin to Marie Antoinette, and from then on Elisabeth Louise's career flourished. By the time she was twenty, she was praised in the *Almanach des Peintres*: "Mlle Vigée is by way of achieving great fame. Full of the desire to excel, she pays great attention to the masters . . . in the art of painting true portraits. Already those she allows out of her atelier are marked by those happy talents. They are composed with taste and are full of feeling; the clothes are beautifully done and the color is strong." Perhaps it helped that M. Lebrun, the writer of these lines, married the artist soon afterward; but most people who saw her work would have agreed that the compliments were deserved.

It wasn't just that Mlle Vigée painted lovely portraits: she was accomplished in many ways. She sang and played the guitar, she dressed simply but well, and she had enormous charm. Soon Mme Geoffrin, Mme du Deffand's great rival, visited her, and she became a regular guest in the salon of the princesse de Rohan-Rochefort. There she met the duc de Choiseul (the former prime minister), the maréchal de Richelieu, and that most elegant of the young bloods, the duc de Lauzun. She painted the comtesse de Brionne—a princess of Lorraine and thus a relation of the

Queen's—and began attending the comtesse's evenings: she had joined the most elegant set in France.

Then, to everyone's horror, Mlle Vigée became the wife of M. Lebrun. It was an arranged marriage, of course. The mean stepfather wanted her out of the house, and poor Elisabeth Louise was glad to go, even if M. Lebrun was in his late thirties and not very attractive. What was worse, he announced that the marriage must be kept secret. An art dealer, he was involved in a business transaction with a Dutch colleague who expected M. Lebrun to marry his own daughter. The Dutchman would certainly break off negotiations if he heard about the wedding. Mlle Vigée complied, but the rumor got around that she was engaged to M. Lebrun, and she had the mortification of being told by all her new friends that Lebrun was a dissolute crook.

"It wasn't that M. Lebrun was a wicked man," she wrote many years later. "His character was a blend of sweetness and liveliness; he was very obliging to everyone; in a word, he was quite pleasing; but his boundless passion for women of low morals, together with his gambling frenzy, caused his ruin and mine." That ruin was altogether imaginary, however. Except for siring a daughter, who was born in 1780, M. Lebrun left his wife free to do as she chose; he simply kept borrowing money from her. Still, Mme Vigée-Lebrun could afford it. Throughout the late seventies and the eighties, she was among the most successful portrait painters in France, able to charge a minimum of 3,500 livres per painting and to earn as much as 70,000 livres ($210,000) a year.

She also gave splendid parties. At first, since her husband used the rest of the house for business, her guests gathered in her large bedroom-sitting room. Soon the press was so great that dukes and marshals of France sat on the floor as the hostess sang and played, or as they listened to the greatest performers of the time. According to that well-informed gossip sheet, the *Mémoires Secrets,*

Mme Lebrun is pretty, she is witty, extremely amiable; all this is more than she needs to attract a brilliant crowd. Recently, she was giving a concert; M. Garat was the singer. MM. de Vaudreuil, de Galliffet, de Polignac, and most of the *agréables* of the court were there. It was on the same evening as the Queen's ball. These gentlemen were agreed that they had a much better time at Mme Lebrun's than at Versailles, that they would stay at her house as long as she pleased and, in fact, they only arrived at Her Majesty's at two or three in the morning, having caused, that night, the festivities to seem less than complete.

The fame of Mme Vigée-Lebrun's concerts, however, was eclipsed by that of her Greek supper. Already on the morning after it, rumor said that millions had been spent to duplicate the feasts of Pericles, that it had been an unspeakable orgy at which all the women were nude. One by one the painter's friends dropped in to ask what had really happened—and how soon she could give another Greek supper. It took a lot of explaining and denying before the truth became clear, but obviously she had filled an unsuspected need: in the middle of the Neoclassical revival, when everyone was engrossed in the Greeks and the Romans, she had brought antiquity to life in Paris itself.

The party, as she quickly explained, had been simple, inexpensive, and improvised. A neighbor had come by to show her his new Etruscan vases, so on the spur of the moment, she decided to have a Greek supper. She borrowed the vases, showed her cook some recipes from *The Travels of Young Anacharsis in Greece* (a current best seller), set up an antique decor in her living room, allowed her hair to stream down her back, and prepared draperies to costume her guests. As for the supper, it was enchanting. The women struck poses inspired by Pompeian frescoes, M. de Cubière played the guitar and pretended it was a lyre, and just as honeycake was passed around, everyone burst into a Gluck chorus entitled "The God of Paphos and Cnidos." Then the doors opened and M. de Vaudreuil, one of the most elegant men in Paris, came in unexpectedly. He was charmed and told everyone about it.

Unlike those other celebrated hostesses, the duchesse de Polignac, the comtesse de Brionne,

Moreau le Jeune. *A Walk in the Woods.* In the late 1770s
and the 1780s, the Bois de Boulogne became the fashionable place
for a late-morning walk or ride. The Metropolitan Museum
of Art, New York. Rogers Fund, 1964 (64.75)

and Mme Necker, Mme Vigée-Lebrun was a working woman who earned every penny she spent.
She was enormously proud of her social accomplishments and recited them at length to her
nephew (who actually wrote her memoirs), but
she never failed to return to the fact that she was
a great portrait painter.

That she was hugely successful is certain.
Commissions came from all the pretty young
women at court and in Paris. Even foreign ladies
passing through France insisted on being painted
by Mme Vigée-Lebrun. Yet to the modern eye,
all this enthusiasm is a little puzzling. As one ex-
amines her canvases, one sees her competence: the
faces are three-dimensional, the skin looks like
skin, the eyes like eyes. The fabrics are convinc-
ingly rendered, the details often charming. However, the personality of the sitter—so visible, for
instance, in David's contemporary portraits—

seems curiously remote. All the women are pretty;
they always smile, but with an artificial smile.
Very quickly, they all begin to look the same.

The artist herself explained this phenomenon: "As I had a horror of the costume that
women wore then, I made great efforts to give
them a more picturesque look. . . . Shawls were
not yet commonly worn but I would arrange wide
scarves, lightly intertwined around the body and
on the arms so as to try and imitate the beautiful
style of the draperies painted by Raphael and
Domenichino. . . . Then, too, I hated hair powder.
I convinced the beautiful duchesse de Gramont-
Caderousse not to wear any when I painted her."
Mme Vigée-Lebrun claims that she herself started
the new fashion of wearing hair powderless and
on the forehead. It may have been all very well in
1780, but for us the result is monotonous and
devoid of information. It would be far more inter-

Moreau le Jeune. *Rendezvous on the Way to Marly.*
These fashionably dressed ladies are on
their way to an afternoon's outing.
The Metropolitan Museum of Art, New York.
Harris Brisbane Dick Fund, 1933 (33.6.11)

Unknown. *Lady in a Garden.* This charming work is typical of the fashion for sentimentality which influenced Mme Vigée-Lebrun. The Metropolitan Museum of Art, New York. Bequest of Susan Dwight Bliss, 1966 (67.55.18)

esting to see how women really looked then.

The clients were pleased, however: being painted in this vaguely Neoclassical style appealed to their sense of fashion. As for their simpering look, Mme Vigée-Lebrun tells us just how it was done: "I tried as hard as I could to give the women I was painting the attitude and expression of their personality; to those who had no personality, and there are quite a few, I tried to give a dreamy look and painted them leaning nonchalantly. They must have been pleased: I could hardly keep up with my commissions; people had trouble getting their names onto my list; in a word, I was in fashion."

Indeed she was. La Harpe, a fashionable intellectual himself, was one of many authors who wrote verses praising the painter:

Le Brun, de la beauté le peintre et le modèle,
Moderne Rosalba, mais plus brillante qu'elle,
Joint la voix de Favart au sourire de Vénus.

("Le Brun, that model and painter of beauty, / That modern, more brilliant Rosalba, / Joins the voice of Favart to the smile of Venus.") And Lebrun (no relation), a poet of immense and justly forgotten fame, delivered himself of a whole eclogue in her praise.

Mme Vigée-Lebrun had pored over Rubens and Van Dyck and learned from them how to paint flesh tones and still lifes. Her bouquets of flowers, for instance, are ravishing. Studying Greuze, she further refined her ability to render beautiful complexions and learned how to paint muslins, white draperies, and velvet. Unfortunately, she also picked up his shallow sentimentality. While she never went in for genre scenes, the soulful expression of her many sitters can be attributed to his influence.

Although Mme Vigée-Lebrun's success was somewhat spoiled by that of a rival, Adélaide Labille-Guiard, she could always count on getting good reviews. The *Journal Général de France,* for instance, wrote of "the richness and brilliance of the color, the grace and originality of the attitudes, the exquisite taste of the clothing which all characterize the extraordinary talents of Mme Le Brun." Perhaps the most cherished compliment that she ever received was given by the husband of the woman who, in 1775, became her favorite model. In anticipation of the deathless "but I know what I like" response to art, Louis XVI looked at the portrait of Marie Antoinette and her children which, to the painter's ineffable contentment, was displayed in the Hall of Mirrors, and exclaimed: "I know nothing about painting, but you make me like it." Mme Vigée-Lebrun had arrived.

It was unavoidable, really: the Queen was mad for fashion and liked being surrounded by pretty women. On both counts, Mme Vigée-Lebrun was an obvious choice. Then there was her ability to paint recognizable but subtly flattering portraits: while people knew they were seeing Marie Antoinette, they also thought that she looked remarkably pretty. From the first sitting, the two women were friends. Marie Antoinette had a taste for music, and Elisabeth Louise's voice was lovely; soon the Queen and the artist were singing duets. And when the portrait was finished, Marie Antoinette took one look and realized that she was seeing the perfect image of herself. From that moment, Mme Vigée-Lebrun was the Queen's painter.

When Maria Theresa received that first Vigée-Lebrun portrait, she too wrote her daughter: "Your big portrait quite delights me. Ligne says it is very like you." This was praise from someone who mattered, and from then on, the artist painted her illustrious model over and over: standing, sitting, in court dress, in garden dress, with her children, holding a rose. As the years passed, of course, the rendition grew increasingly flattering. The heavy lower lip narrowed, the double chin vanished, the heavy bosom shrank. As a result, those portraits tell us remarkably little about what the Queen actually looked like. For all the acres of canvas that Mme Vigée-Lebrun covered, it is to a sketch by Kucharsky that we must go if we want to see the real Marie Antoinette.

Mme Vigée-Lebrun's relationship with the Queen was just as important to her as the portraits, for it crowned both of her careers, artistic and social. The memoirs are full of little anec-

Moreau le Jeune. *A Perfect Harmony.*
The Metropolitan Museum of Art, New York.
The Lesley and Emma Sheafer Collection,
Bequest of Emma A. Sheafer, 1973 (1974.356.48)

Mme Vigée-Lebrun. *Madame
Grant, Later princesse de Talleyrand.*
"To those who had no personality, . . .
I tried to give a dreamy look."
The Metropolitan Museum of Art, New York.
Bequest of Edward S. Harkness, 1940 (50.135.2)

dotes about the gracious sovereign. There was the time, for instance, when the pregnant Elisabeth Louise was too unwell to come to Versailles for a sitting. Trembling for fear she had given offense, she went the next day and was told by an underling that there was no question of having a sitting with the Queen. Her Majesty was just going for a drive; the carriage was ready and waiting. The poor artist was preparing to go home again when the Queen appeared on her way out. Mme Vigée-Lebrun tells us:

> My heart was beating fast, and I felt all the more afraid that I was in the wrong. The Queen turned to me and said in a kind voice, "I waited for you all morning yesterday. What happened to you?"
>
> "Alas, Madam," I answered, "I was so ill that I could not attend Your Majesty. I have come today for Your Majesty's orders and will return to Paris instantly."
>
> "No, no, don't go," said the Queen, "I won't have you come all this way for nothing." She sent the carriage away and prepared to sit for me. I remember that I was so anxious to deserve this kind treatment that I picked up my paintbox too fast and it tipped over. "Leave it, leave it," the Queen said, "you are too far along in your pregnancy to bend down," and, despite anything I could say, she picked up everything herself.

This was an extraordinary gesture from a monarch whose very gloves were handed to her on a gold plate.

Of course, the sovereign did what she could to advance the career of her favorite painter. It had long been a thorn in Mme Vigée-Lebrun's side that she was unable to belong to the Academy because her husband was an art dealer. She often protested that she herself had nothing to do with M. Lebrun's business, but the law said that husband and wife were one. It was the perfect pretext to keep out someone whose success had made many of her colleagues jealous. In 1783, however, the Queen spoke to the King, who spoke to the minister in charge, who said that the Academy's rules were strict and there was nothing to be done. So the King went back to the Queen; they had another talk; and the minister was made to understand where his duty lay. Within the

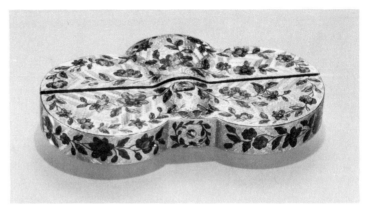

Spectacle case, Paris.
The Metropolitan Museum of Art, New York.
Gift of Mr. and Mrs. Charles Wrightsman, 1976 (1976.155.168)

Gold and enamel snuffbox, French.
The Metropolitan Museum of Art, New York.
Gift of Mr. and Mrs. Charles Wrightsman, 1976 (1976.155.5)

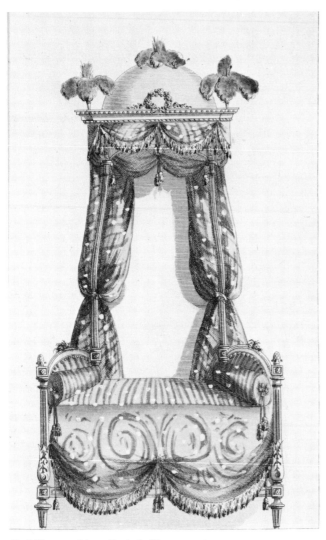

Bed illustrated in a Paris fashion magazine,
Le Cabinet des Modes. The Metropolitan Museum of Art,
New York. Harris Brisbane Dick Fund, 1938 (38.38.6)

month Mme Vigée-Lebrun had become an acade-
mician, though not without a snide comment
in the Academy's register: "The Academy, deferring with the deepest respect to its Sovereign's
orders. . . ."

The new distinction carried a major advantage: from then on, Mme Vigée-Lebrun could
exhibit her work in the Academy's yearly Salon.
In 1783, along with a portrait of Mme Grant,
a ravishing demimondaine, she decided to send
in a big set piece entitled *Peace Brings Back
Abundance* to show that she was no mere portrait
painter. In this canvas the two large women who
sit on either side of a cornucopia are, unfortunately, of mixed parentage: their size and lushness
are Rubenesque, while their position and blank
expressions are Neoclassical. Although the work as
a whole looks thoroughly silly, there are the usual
redeeming graces of Mme Vigée-Lebrun's competence. The color is lush and vibrant, the cornucopia is an attractive still life in itself, the draperies
are full of sensual realism. And as usual, the work
was well received.

Mme Vigée-Lebrun's next entry in the Salon,
however, caused such a scandal that it had to be
withdrawn. It was a portrait of Marie Antoinette
wearing a fashionable linen shift called a *gaulle.*
"Many people," one critic wrote, "have found it
offensive to see these august persons revealed to
the public wearing clothes reserved for the privacy
of their palace." People who hated Marie Antoinette—and by 1784 they were legion—accused
her of wanting to ruin the Lyons silk industry by
wearing English linens. Besides, they said, you
could see that a queen who dressed like a shop-
keeper was capable of anything.

In 1785 Mme Vigée-Lebrun was commissioned to paint a large, official portrait of the
Queen and her children. The purpose was strictly
political: the sovereign, seated in her state bedroom, would be shown in all the pomp of royalty,
while the children would underline her success at
the crucial task of providing an heir to the throne.
So aware was she of the painting's importance
that Mme Vigée-Lebrun spent almost two years
on it. The composition is borrowed from one of
Raphael's madonnas, and except for the fact that

Mme Vigée-Lebrun (attributed to). *Marie Antoinette Wearing a "Gaulle."*
This scandalous portrait had to be hastily withdrawn from the Salon.
National Gallery of Art, Washington, D.C. Timken Collection

Marie Antoinette looks about ten years younger than she was, the work is an undoubted success. In it the Queen is appropriately grand, imposing, yet maternal. Still, by then her unpopularity was so great that at first, Mme Vigée-Lebrun pretended the painting wasn't ready. The Salon opened without it, and the empty frame was promptly dubbed *Portrait of a Deficit* in allusion to Marie Antoinette's nickname of Madame Déficit. When the painting of the spendthrift Queen finally appeared, it received mixed reviews.

Commissions still poured in so profusely that the artist raised her price to 12,000 livres ($36,000) a picture. In spite of the sums that M. Lebrun borrowed and squandered, she had become very well-to-do and was buying a new house. She was in a position to enjoy that ease of living which died with the Revolution. Later she wrote sadly:

> No one can understand what society was like in France who hasn't lived in that era when, once all the day's business was done, twelve or fifteen amiable people gathered at a lady's house to spend the evening together. Their ease, their gaiety, their good temper . . . gave [those suppers] a charm that a dinner can never have. A sort of intimate trust united the guests; and since people with good manners can always freely dispense with formalities, it was in its suppers that Paris society revealed itself superior to that of the rest of Europe. . . . People were cheerful, they were amiable, the hours fled like minutes.

Soon, however, Mme Vigée-Lebrun was watching the people marching instead of the aristocrats supping, and she did not hesitate. Like most of her clients, she promptly fled the Revolution. Unlike them, she did quite as well abroad as she had done at home.

Taking her daughter but leaving her husband behind, Mme Vigée-Lebrun set off on October 5, 1789, just as the King and Queen were dragged back from Versailles to Paris by a screaming mob. She stopped in Florence for a few days, then moved on to Rome, where she met Angelica Kauffmann, another highly successful woman painter. She was received by the French ambassador, the cardinal de Bernis, Mme de Pompadour's erstwhile minis-

ter of war. She exhibited a self-portrait and instantly became the rage. "I would seem vain if I told you all the details of [the self-portrait's] success," she wrote the artist Hubert Robert. "It has gone so far that never in my life have I received this kind of encouragement. . . . All the artists have visited, *revisited,* along with princesses from every nation. . . . I am receiving highly laudatory verse." Commissions came in as copiously as in France, and Elisabeth Louise was made a member of the Accademia di San Lucca.

After a while Mme Vigée-Lebrun once again felt the pull of royalty. Marie Antoinette was no longer accessible, but her sister, Maria Carolina, ruled over Naples and Sicily. So off the painter went, to produce more royal portraits and meet the famous Lady Hamilton. Then she returned to clients in Rome, but the Revolution was reaching all the way to St. Peter's, and the Pope's position began to look as shaky as that of poor Louis XVI. So Mme Vigée-Lebrun was off once more, to Vienna, where again acclaim and commissions awaited her. It was there that in the midst of a round of parties she heard about Marie Antoinette's death. She learned of the execution about two weeks late, for since she couldn't bear bad news, she had refused to read the newspapers or talk about current events.

Austria was agreeable, but farther north lay a land of gold and ice that was happily short of portrait painters. In 1795 Mme Vigée-Lebrun moved on to Russia, where she was received by Catherine II and the rest of the imperial family. The Empress immediately commissioned a painting of her granddaughters, but for once the artist failed to please. The practical Empress took a look at the portrait and declared it silly, undignified, and sentimental.

Luckily for Elisabeth Louise, everyone else was charmed with her painting. The Grand Duchess Elizabeth, wife of the future Czar Alexander I, promptly ordered her portrait, and the rest of Saint Petersburg soon followed. Mme Vigée-Lebrun charged as much as 15,000 rubles per painting and was a frequent guest in all the grandest houses. There she was reunited with many of her Paris friends who, having emigrated to Russia, were trying hard to recreate their salons.

As for Mme Vigée-Lebrun's style of painting, it remained unchanged except for a slight tendency toward more realism. The formula she had evolved in Paris—the scarf, the natural look, the sentimental expression—was repeated over and over. And no one seemed to mind: in 1800 Mme Vigée-Lebrun was made a member of the Russian Academy of Fine Arts.

Still, she missed Paris and—having been taken off the list of emigrés, owing to M. Lebrun's efforts—decided to go home. Alexander I, who was now czar, begged her to stay—so she did, for three more months.

Then she set off, stopping in Berlin to paint the royal family (a king is a king, after all), and arrived home in January, 1802. She found the new Paris a thorough disappointment, however. It wasn't that she had been forgotten; on the contrary, she was admirably received; but everything had changed. There were no more salons, no more manners, no more court at Versailles. Mme Vigée-Lebrun was so disgruntled that she even deplored the disappearance of powdered hair; she had come a long way since the eighties. So she went over to England and was received by the comte d'Artois, Louis XVI's youngest brother, as well as by all the best English society. Still, it wasn't Paris; but when she came home this time, she found herself in disfavor. Napoleon didn't like royalists, and the political lines were hardening.

She still went on painting—a portrait of Mme de Staël, Swiss landscapes—but her drive was ebbing. She bought herself a pleasant house in Louveciennes and retired there in comfort. Then the event she had been longing for actually occurred: in 1814 the Bourbons regained their throne. Of course she was received by Louis XVIII and the comte d'Artois whom, after all, she had painted in their youth at Versailles. And history repeated itself; once more she was commissioned to paint royal portraits. After a while, she realized that she was getting old—she was sixty-seven in 1820—and settled down in Louveciennes for good. She was rich, respected, surrounded by loving nephews and nieces. By the time she died in 1842, people had forgotten all about her, but it no longer seemed to matter. Young Mlle Vigée had achieved her ends. She had known artistic renown, financial ease, and social success: now Mme Vigée-Lebrun could die in peace.

To Rule a World

The margravine of Bayreuth
Queen Maria Carolina

Civilization, the Romans thought, stopped at the Rhine; beyond the river wild tribesmen fought obscure wars, worshiped peculiar gods, and behaved in repulsive ways. By the beginning of the eighteenth century, some states in Germany, at least, seemed to have progressed: Bavaria was one, Austria another. The farther east you went, however, the more likely you were to run into odd, barbaric customs. This was particularly the case in Europe's newest kingdom, Prussia.

There has been a good deal of debate about the nature of Prussia before 1866, but prior to Frederick II's reign, there can be none at all. A land of bleak plains and marshes, small, dirty towns, and a large army, Prussia had very little to recommend it except brute strength. Even then it was at best a secondary power.

As for the new King of Prussia, Frederick William I, he was known to be incredibly bad-tempered and uncivilized. His principal occupation was to make the people around him suffer, his family most of all. The Queen, the court, and the royal family lived in terror. Frederick William was not just irascible, but physically violent as well. He beat up his children so often and so severely that his oldest daughter, Wilhelmina, never fully recovered from her injuries. If any children today were treated half as badly as the princes and princesses of Prussia, they would be instantly removed from their parents' control; in Berlin early in the eighteenth century, the Queen could only watch and endure.

That the children survived at all is a miracle of sorts. Luckily the servants pitied them and helped when they could; otherwise Their Royal Highnesses might literally have died of starvation. "We only lived on coffee and dried cherries," Wilhelmina wrote in her memoirs, "and that completely ruined the digestion. . . . The King behaved like a butler; he served everyone except for my brother and myself and when, by any chance, there was food left over in the dish, he

Pesne. *Wilhelmina, Margravine of Bayreuth.*
Photograph courtesy of Galerie Fischer, Lucerne

would spit in it to prevent us taking any. . . .
I was fed on insults and invective for I was called
by every name imaginable, all day and in front
of everyone." The Queen was not allowed to see
her children, so whenever the King went hunting,
she would post servants at the windows to watch
for his return—then she would send for Frederick
and Wilhelmina. Once the watchers slipped up,
so Frederick had to hide in the closet where the
Queen's *chaise percée* was kept, while Wilhelmina
crept, with great difficulty because there was so
little space, under the Queen's bed.

It wasn't that the King hated everybody. He
liked his generals, provided they got drunk with
him, and his army. He had strict standards for his
soldiers: they must be at least six feet tall and
very strong. He also enjoyed accumulating money,
and the more he had, the more certain he was
that he didn't want to spend any. His occupations
were simple: he looked after his army, he hunted,
and he drank. He also knew what he disliked: his
family; anything to do with books, art, or culture; anything that cost money; and the world
outside Prussia. Whenever he encountered any
of these irritants, he dealt with it swiftly: he beat
his children, forbade everyone to read books, and
refused to part with his cash.

All in all, this did not make for a pleasant
life if you were related to Frederick William. It
seemed as if Wilhelmina, in particular, would
not live through childhood. However, her first
and nasty governess was replaced by Frau von
Sonsfeld, who turned out to be so kind and so
helpful that many years later Wilhelmina wrote:
"She is still with me and it looks as if only death
will separate us." Besides being a nice woman,
Frau von Sonsfeld noticed that her pupil was unusually bright. She encouraged Wilhelmina to
study as a means of escaping the dreadful life she
led, and through the years the child secretly became a cultivated woman, educated in history,
philosophy, music, literature, and languages. Like
her brother Frederick, she spoke French, read
French—even wrote French so fluently, so styl-
ishly that the nineteenth-century critic Sainte-
Beuve numbered her among the great French
writers.

Luckily too, she had the companionship of
her brother. Both Frederick and Wilhelmina were
extraordinarily intelligent, loved books, music,
and the arts, cared about the world outside Prussia, and perhaps more important, stood united
against the King. "Never has there been tenderness to equal ours," Wilhelmina wrote. As for
Frederick, that fierce anti-Catholic, he put it another way: "I am as close to you, my amiable sister, as the Pope is to the Devil." To the end of
their lives, brother and sister continued to write,
visit, and love each other.

By 1729 Wilhelmina was twenty-one: it was
time she was married. The Queen, who had an
eye for glamour, persuaded the King to arrange a
double alliance in which Wilhelmina would marry
George I's grandson and heir presumptive, while
Frederick would marry Princess Ann of Glouces-
ter. Then the King thought better of it; an English princess would be a nuisance at his court. So
that was off. The next candidate, Augustus of
Saxony, King of Poland, was over fifty years old,
"known for his debauchery, and a hopeless drunk,"
Wilhelmina wrote. Being as obstinate as she was
downtrodden, she doggedly resisted the match.

By then the princess was "one of the hand-
somest women in Germany, tall, with a wonderful
figure and an air of dignity which makes her position immediately visible," according to the German traveler Pollnitz. Still, she was now twenty-
two and unmarried. The English match seemed
to revive briefly, then founder. In despair the
Queen proposed a new candidate, a distant
relative: the son and heir of the margrave of
Bayreuth.

The King was disgusted. The prospective
groom had neither money nor power; Bayreuth
was a tiny, unimportant state; worse, it was thoroughly unmilitary. This time the Queen insisted,
so Frederick William agreed to the match but refused to provide a dowry or even attend the wedding. To give him some polish before he became a
husband, young Bayreuth was sent off by his
father on an educational trip. There, for a while,
things rested.

Then the world of the Prussian court exploded. Frederick, who had been consistently

mistreated by his father because he liked to read and play the flute, and because he was heir to the throne, decided to run away. The King found out and took action. He wrote the Queen: "I have had that scoundrel of a Fritz arrested. I shall treat him as his crime and his cowardice deserve. I no longer own him for my son; he has dishonored all my house; such a wretch does not deserve to live." Both mother and daughter, knowing the King's love of violence, felt sure that Frederick was dead. In fact, the King merely had Frederick's best friend shot as the prince was forced to watch.

The next scene, as described by Wilhelmina and confirmed by eyewitnesses, took place at court. She writes:

> We all ran to kiss [the King's] hands, but directly he saw me, his face changed and anger and rage seized his heart. He turned black in the face, his face flushed with fury, and he foamed at the mouth.
>
> "Infamous scum," he yelled, "you dare to show yourself before me? Go keep your villain of a brother company!" With which he seized me by one hand and struck me several blows in the face with his fist; one hit me so violently on the temple that I fell back and should have split my skull on the wainscot, had not Frau von Sonsfeld caught me by my headdress and broken the force of the fall.

After dragging his daughter around by her hair, the King ordered her confined to her room. For the next three weeks she was bedridden from her injuries. At least word was passed to her that Frederick was still alive, a captive in a dark cell at the fortress of Küstrin. As the weeks dragged on, Wilhelmina remained a prisoner in her room, though after a while Frau von Sonsfeld was allowed to attend her. Finally after almost a year of confinement, her father's chancellor informed her that she would be released if she agreed to marry young Bayreuth immediately. Her mother, whom she was now allowed to see, had new hopes for the English weddings and strongly opposed the match with Bayreuth. As usual, however, the King won.

On November 20, 1731, Wilhelmina became the prospective margravine of Bayreuth. It wasn't much of a position, but at least she liked her husband. Frederick, prince of Bayreuth, she wrote, was

> . . . tall and well built . . . with a noble expression, neither handsome nor ugly but with an open, pleasant, agreeable expression which made up for his lack of beauty. He seemed lively, had always a ready repartee, and was never shy. . . . He was very cheerful, his conversation was pleasant although he had some trouble expressing himself because he stutered so badly. The kindness of his heart brought him the love of all who knew him. . . . His only shortcoming was a certain lack of seriousness; he didn't like to do anything which required [mental] effort . . . and spent his time in children's games.

Wilhelmina fell in love with him just as he was, and they went off to Bayreuth with the best of expectations.

These were swiftly disappointed, however. The current margrave of Bayreuth, George Frederick, was an amiable and cultivated man who was so fond of watches that he carried one in every pocket. On the whole he led a quiet life, having just been forced to repudiate his wife for gross and spectacular adultery. Like most German princes, of course, he got drunk twice a day, but unlike the King of Prussia, he wasn't violent. The principality of Bayreuth had been almost bankrupt when he inherited it from a spendthrift cousin. After selling off the plate, the jewelry, and most of the furniture he found in the several far too grand palaces built by his predecessor, he proceeded to spend as little money as possible for the rest of his life.

What this meant, Wilhelmina swiftly discovered, was that her rooms in the Residenz were a shambles. Most of the windowpanes were broken or missing—and German winters are very cold indeed. The walls were covered with filth, the bed-curtains were so old that they disintegrated when the princess tried to close them, and there were no chairs, tables, stools, or other necessary furniture. As for the food, it was not only bad but insufficient. Since the margrave was not about to give his son any money, nothing could be fixed.

Even worse, the princess had to cope with a

grotesquely complex court etiquette and endure unpleasantness all around because she was a royal highness while the margrave was only a plain highness. (To us the difference may seem almost invisible, but anyone in a German court before the First World War would cheerfully have killed in order to rise from mere highness-ship to the exalted rank of the royals.) The women at court were also a shock to Wilhelmina. She writes:

> Imagine monsters with coiffures shaped like chestnuts, or rather swallow's wings, their hairpieces full of dirt and garbage; their clothes were as antique as those of their husbands. Fifty ribbon bows, in every color, were added on for greater luster. Their curtsies were awkward: I have never seen anything more comical. . . . The ladies were as unpleasant as the men. I found myself in the company of thirty-four drunks who had had so much liquor they were unable even to speak. . . . Having had enough of watching them throw up, I finally got up and left the room, not much impressed by these beginnings.

Life was no better outside the palace. The town had a population of six thousand, none of whom went out at night because there were no streetlights. The townspeople looked shabby not because, like the margrave, they were parsimonious, but because they had no money. "I found myself in a new world," the princess wrote sadly, "with people who were peasants more than courtiers." By comparison even Berlin seemed like a metropolis.

There was one great consolation: Wilhelmina and her husband were really in love. Also, they did have interests in common. They both spoke French all the time, and they loved music and played flute duos. Besides, the athletic prince seems to have been attractive and sexy. Early in 1732 the old margrave relented and gave the princess a little palace, the Hermitage, which had been built by his predecessor. It was a charming building, with staterooms and greenhouses, surrounded by a large, ornate park—altogether an improvement on the crumbling Residenz.

The first thing Wilhelmina did in her new palace was to put on a play; in the eighteenth century, life without the theater was hardly worth living. Bayreuth was fanatically Protestant, however, and the ministers were scandalized. They complained to the margrave, who in turn called in his daughter-in-law and made a scene. The old man became so unpleasant that Wilhelmina decided to return to Berlin for a while, but she lacked the money for the trip. After she had arranged to borrow it from the servants, she found that she was pregnant and couldn't go. When she finally revisited Berlin, it was alone. Her husband, who found himself forced to serve in the Prussian army, was posted to a garrison. During her stay Frederick William was his usual odious self; the Queen was difficult; only Frederick (free now from his confinement) was pleasant, but he had to be careful.

In 1733 Wilhelmina's situation in Bayreuth worsened. Her husband was off with the Prussian army fighting in the War of the Polish Succession, and she was terrified that he would be killed. The margrave grew increasingly difficult. To Wilhelmina's horror, she discovered that Frau von Sonsfeld's sister, Flore, had become his mistress and was planning to marry him. The scandal would have been immense. Ruling princes were supposed to marry only into other ruling families; besides, he might have more children. Astonishingly, when Wilhelmina appealed to her, Flore von Sonsfeld agreed not to marry the margrave no matter how often he asked. This was an incredibly selfless act; after all, marriage would have meant an enormous rise in status. Even more incredible, Flore von Sonsfeld actually talked the margrave into being nicer to Wilhelmina.

Still, it was a great relief to the young Bayreuths when the margrave died in May, 1735. Immediately everything changed, for the new margrave started spending money. He gave his wife clothes, jewelry, books—all the luxuries she had had to do without. He began improving and enlarging the Hermitage; the park was almost doubled in size; musicians were brought in; court etiquette was changed to conform to French customs.

For the first time in her life, Wilhelmina found herself actually happy. She felt so well, in fact, that she even tried hunting with her husband, but she soon stopped because she hated killing animals. She was fond of her dog Folichon in particular, and conducted a correspondence on his behalf with Biche, Frederick's little bitch in Berlin. A letter signed "Biche" said:

> The great tenderness that my master feels for your mistress has convinced me to love only one dog. Yes, Folichon, I have decided to accept your sweet paw in marriage.

To which Folichon answered:

> You and I, my dear Biche, understand the world. . . . Are we not similar to men in every way? Love, jealousy, anger, gluttony rule us and them as well and, if indeed there is any difference between us, it is simply that we have far fewer vices and many more virtues. Men are frivolous, inconstant, greedy, ambitious. We are not afflicted by these failings. On the other hand, we exemplify faithfulness, constancy, devotion, and gratitude, all qualities hardly to be found in human society.

All her life, often with good reason, the margravine took the bleak view of human nature that she expresses here.

Though life was still difficult in Berlin—Frederick William, after all, lived on until May, 1740—at Bayreuth everything had been transformed as if by a magic wand. Fetes, banquets, ballets filled the margravine's blissful days. The Hermitage was redecorated in the current Rococo style. There were boiseries and mirrors, a Japanese room, a Chinese room—all light, cheerful, charming. In the new, larger park, fountains and ponds appeared everywhere. A Temple of Silence dedicated to the Muses was built, along with a charming little theater. In addition to the court's official festivities, the margravine gave smaller, wonderfully luxurious parties for a few selected guests.

Wilhelmina also assembled a "pretty little library which," according to Voltaire, "she puts to good use." Concert followed concert, often with the margravine herself demonstrating her considerable talent for the flute. She tried to create a salon, that ambition of any intelligent eighteenth-century woman, but there she failed. There was no one in Bayreuth capable of conversing in a civilized manner.

Wilhelmina's new opulence was partly spoiled for her by ill health: she had remained

Wille. *Frederick II*. The Metropolitan Museum of Art, New York. Gift of Georgiana W. Sargent, in memory of John Osborne Sargent, 1924 (24.63.10)

fragile ever since that dreadful childhood. Now one disorder came after the other. In 1737 she was so ill that Frederick had to persuade the margrave to give the King of Prussia two tall soldiers in exchange for a French doctor.

Brother and sister remained as close as ever. Soon after Frederick William died, the new King of Prussia visited the margravine. Although he became quite difficult when he was actually with her, he wrote as soon as he left: "I thank you a thousand times for the friendship and tenderness you showed me during my stay at the Hermitage and hope you will sometimes, in your moments of leisure, remember a brother who loves you tenderly and will remain devoted and faithful to you his whole life through."

This brother, soon to be known as Frederick the Great, was in a position to give his sister the thing she craved most: a contact with the French intelligentsia. In the fall of 1740, he invited Wilhelmina to come and stay with him at Rheinsberg, just outside Berlin. Not only did he pay for the trip, a great proof of love, but he introduced her to the dazzling Voltaire himself. The visit was everything Wilhelmina had dreamed of: the master's new play was in rehearsals, there were chamber music concerts in which the brother and sister were reunited, and best of all, there was the kind of sparkling conversation—in French, naturally—for which Voltaire was justly famous.

Her idyll at Rheinsberg ended in January, 1741, because Frederick II was off to conquer Silesia, but Wilhelmina's friendship with Voltaire lasted as long as her life. That the margravine should have admired him was hardly surprising. On his part Voltaire, although he was fond of royal highnesses, would have dropped Wilhelmina in haste if he had found her dull or stupid. Instead, he wrote when he heard that she was ill again, "Your Royal Highness and the King, your brother, have, I think, of all princes the best wit and the worse stomach: everything must have its compensation." And during a visit to Bayreuth three years later, he said: "I have seen a court where all the pleasures of society and of the mind are freely offered. We have had operas, plays, hunts, delicious suppers. . . . Bayreuth is a retreat where one may enjoy all the advantages of a court without the inconveniences of grandeur."

Even as this visit proceeded, the margravine's new opera house was beginning to rise. Sensibly, she had sent for an Italian architect and stage designer, the famous Giuseppe Bibiena. By 1746 she was able to inaugurate the most ravishing of Rococo theaters by listening to her own singers. Soon French actors were hired, chief among them that Le Kain whom Mlle Clairon so loathed. The burghers of Bayreuth, who knew that the margravine didn't like to see empty seats, found themselves forced to spend evenings watching perfectly incomprehensible goings-on.

Meanwhile between 1744 and 1747, Wilhelmina found herself at odds with the two people she loved best: her brother and her husband. When she had left Berlin years before as a new bride, the princess had brought with her two rich sisters, the Misses von Marwitz. Now, Prussian law forbade the marriage of any Prussian girl with property to a foreigner. When, however, Wilhelmina found out that the eldest Marwitz girl had become the margrave's mistress, she decided to marry the girl off within the month. Since the only available candidate was Austrian, the famous law was broken. The margrave was none too pleased to lose his mistress, although being good-tempered, he was soon reconciled with his wife. Frederick II, on the other hand, was furious because his sister had deliberately broken the law. To make it all worse, a newspaper in the little town of Erlanger, which was part of the margraviate, published articles backing Maria Theresa, Frederick's enemy in the War of the Austrian Succession. The King became truly enraged. He went on writing his sister, but in the coldest, most distant way.

At last, however, Wilhelmina's stream of apologies softened him, and the reconciliation between brother and sister was deep and permanent. "You have every kind of intelligence, every kind of talent, and every kind of knowledge," Frederick wrote her. "You can discuss coiffures, wars, politics, talk about the most sublime philosophy or the most frivolous novel, and nothing is alien to you. I should tell you more about how friendly

I feel toward you, but you know all about it, and I don't want to bore you with the feeling which makes me so happy." In truth, Wilhelmina was the only woman for whom this thorough misogynist felt anything but contempt.

From 1747 on, while the margravine's health deteriorated steadily, she built a new Hermitage in which there was a conservatory with painted, sculpted stucco walls decorated with fruit-laden orange and peach trees inhabited by exotic birds. At the back of the room, a fountain sprang from a shell supported by two dolphins; behind it one could glimpse a grotto inlaid with multicolored crystals. The concerts, carrousels, and banquets continued as ever. So did the correspondence with Voltaire, though now it took a melancholy tone. "We have a great need to fill the gaps in the conversation," the margravine wrote. "Our discussions sound to me like Chinese music: long pauses end in discordant tones." And since Voltaire wouldn't settle in Bayreuth, she begged him at least to send a friend; then perhaps she could have a salon.

After that, it was all downhill. A trip to France and Italy in 1754 was pleasant enough, but the margravine felt that she wasn't getting the attention she deserved. And indeed, who cared about a little German princess? Then the Seven Years War started, and at first Frederick endured defeat after defeat. In an attempt to be of help, Wilhelmina started an elaborate negotiation through Voltaire with the maréchal de Richelieu, who commanded one of the French armies. Nothing came of it, and she wrote: "Europe suffers, Prussia deserves pity. I am in a dreadful state and will not survive the destruction of my House and family: that is the only consolation remaining to me."

Frederick's victory at Rossbach over the maréchal de Soubise, Mme de Pompadour's friend, was a comfort to Wilhelmina. Her brother's position was still precarious, however, and she worried. In the summer of 1758 she grew so much sicker that Frederick wrote her: "If I lose you, the loss will be irreparable for me." Not even his encouragement could help: on October 14, 1758, the margravine was dead.

Ombre illustre, ombre chère, âme héroïque et pure
Toi que mes tristes yeux ne cessent de pleurer.

("Illustrious shade, beloved shade, pure and heroic soul/You for whom, from sad eyes, my tears flow ever on.") So Voltaire wrote in one of his less successful odes, while Frederick, for the first and only time in his life, really mourned. Sobbing for days on end, he wrote Voltaire: "You can easily judge of my sorrow by the loss I have endured. Some catastrophes can be overcome by constancy and a little courage; but there are others against which all the firmness with which one tries to arm oneself and the speeches of the philosophers are an empty and useless help."

As for the margrave, he does not seem to have missed his wife much; at any rate, he was soon remarried. Of course, he was no intellectual like Frederick and Voltaire. Both of these men had their failings, not least of which was an extraordinary self-absorption. Still, they were able to appreciate the remarkable achievements of this princess who, despite a bitter childhood and the cultural poverty of tiny Bayreuth, participated in the great explosion of taste and intelligence that was occurring in western Europe. Because of that, and because she was a free, tolerant, and generous spirit, she deserves to be remembered today along with her more illustrious contemporaries.

Queen Maria Carolina

The empress Maria Theresa was a devoted mother. She loved her children, dealt with them strictly, watched over their education, and made sure they were among the most accomplished princes and princesses of their generation. When they reached their teens, she taught them that they were tools in a vast political scheme. Their happiness, she made clear, must henceforth lie in being model monarchs and, no matter what throne they occupied, good Austrians.

An austere childhood may not be the best preparation for confronting royal temptations, or long-distance patriotism the best path to local popularity. In any event, as queens the Empress's daughters Marie Antoinette and Maria Carolina were known for their wild, extravagant lives and the hatred they aroused in their subjects.

The two sisters shared a sense of enormous pride and self-worth: not only were they Hapsburgs, but they were daughters of the great Maria Theresa. The conviction that they were born to rule was strengthened as soon as they met their husbands. Neither the future Louis XVI nor Ferdinand IV of Naples was able to impress a lively, well-educated, self-important princess. As long as Maria Theresa lived, her frequent letters from Vienna exerted some sort of control over her daughters. After her death in 1780, they were left to follow their own judgment, and no one except an aroused people could stop them.

Their model education had anticipated nineteenth-century repressiveness, for the Empress had made sure that her children were denied whatever they wanted most. The result was that they indulged themselves endlessly when given the chance; after all, they had a lot of catching up to do. Of course, that applied only to the ones who got away: the archduchess Josepha was not so lucky. She had been promised to the King of Naples, but despite her frantic pleas, the Empress made her come on a visit to the crypt where all the Hapsburgs were buried. There in an open coffin lay a relative freshly dead of smallpox. Josepha, having obeyed her mother, caught the disease and died.

Fortunately, Maria Theresa had so many daughters that one more or less didn't matter. Maria Carolina was now assigned to Josepha's fiancé—to her fury, for she had aspired to a much more glamorous match with the Dauphin. She was given no choice; in 1768 she was packed off to Naples.

At sixteen Maria Carolina looked fresh and pleasing. She was intelligent, knowledgeable in history and philosophy, fluent in French and Italian, and polished in manners. She had been taught to expect the same achievements in all royalty, and as she moved through Italy, people who knew her fiancé were apprehensive. "She is a most amiable little Queen," Horace Mann wrote Walpole from Florence, "but it is to be feared that her extreme delicacy and good sense will only make her feel the more the want of it in her Royal consort." That was putting it mildly.

Ferdinand IV, in fact, had reached the age of seventeen in a state of such deep ignorance that even his uncultivated court was shocked. He knew nothing, but was convinced that he knew everything by virtue of being King. He never read anything if he could help it and had such difficulty in signing his name that a stamp was made to spare him the exertion. He hated washing, couldn't bear to be alone, and spoke the roughest kind of Neapolitan dialect. Still, he did have two desirable qualities: he was healthy, and he had been born in Naples.

Naples and Sicily had long been ruled by either Spanish or Austrian viceroys, depending on the fortunes of war. Then in 1738 they became the property of Don Carlos de Borbón, the youngest son of Philip V of Spain. This was already a huge improvement. Not only did a resident king and court create a new cultural atmosphere, but also the kingdom enjoyed greater prosperity now that tax revenues were spent on the spot instead of being sent off to Madrid or Vienna. When Don Carlos inherited the throne of Spain in 1759, he left his second son behind as King of Naples and took his other children to Madrid with him.

Mengs. *Queen Maria Carolina.*
Photograph issued and authorized by
the Patrimonio Nacional, Madrid

Saint Non. *View of Naples,* a plate from *Voyage pittoresque.*
General Research Division, The New York Public Library,
Astor, Lenox and Tilden Foundations

Ferdinand was only eight years old, however, and Don Carlos left his own chief minister, the marchese Tanucci, as head of the regency council. Tanucci proved a competent prime minister and a faithful servant. Every week a long letter went to Madrid telling Charles III about current problems and asking for his decisions. Every week a letter came back from Spain carrying precise instructions.

As for Ferdinand, Don Carlos entrusted his education to a Neapolitan nobleman, the prince of San Nicandro. Sensible of this great advantage, the prince decided that he would make himself loved, and thus gain favor, by never forcing Ferdinand to do anything he didn't want to do. The results were appalling. William Hamilton, the British minister, wrote in March, 1767:

> His Sicilian Majesty . . . has neither had masters capable of instructing him nor governors who have studied to inspire him with ideas worthy of his rank. He is loved from the vulgar Neapolitans merely from having been born amongst them and if he loves them, as he seems to do, it is perhaps that by the distance they have always carefully placed between him and the nobility of his own age, he has been drove rather to seek the company of menial servants and people of the very lowest class.

In consequence, Ferdinand felt at ease only when surrounded with servants, and physical exercise was his only diversion. He rode, hunted, and fished. He was good with his hands. When he went fishing, he liked to sell his catch in the market for the best price possible, then give the money away. His idea of a joke was to tickle his courtiers, or cause them to slip and fall, or chase them with a freshly filled and stinking chamberpot. He did not doubt that this was the proper behavior for a king because he had met with nothing but approval ever since he could remember.

Though he was a rude shock for poor Maria Carolina, she did her best. She had not come to Naples to enjoy herself, but to gain another ally for Austria. Her mother had stipulated in the marriage contract that the new Queen would be admitted to the council of state as soon as she had given birth to an heir. For the moment, there was little she could achieve. Tanucci and Charles III still ran the government, and Ferdinand was quite convinced of his own incapacity to do so. While she waited for an heir, however, she could at least gain control over her husband.

At first the courtiers were convinced that she would fail. After the wedding night, Ferdinand rose early and went hunting, as usual. When he was asked how he had found Maria Carolina, he answered: "Dorme comm'un amazzata e suda comm'un porco" ("She sleeps like a dead woman and sweats like a pig"). Within a matter of months, however, he had come to recognize his wife's superiority. All too conscious that he knew nothing (by now San Nicandro was in the deepest disgrace), he began to think that she knew everything.

That Maria Carolina was intelligent cannot be doubted. Another sixteen-year-old might have asserted her superiority and made an enemy of the King. Instead she behaved with immense tact. She hated to hunt, but she went with Ferdinand and praised him. She laughed at his jokes, showed him the proper respect, and allowed him to realize by himself that things were better left to his wife. Then too, in a court occupied only with sex and pleasure, the young Queen managed to remain dignified, pleasant, and virtuous. All in all, the King was impressed.

"Er ist ein recht guter Narr" ("He is a right good fool"), the Queen commented to her brother, the emperor Joseph II, who had come to see for himself. The Emperor agreed, but wrote, "Although an ugly prince, he is not absolutely repulsive." He added, "He loves his country and admires it to excess, believing that all he has is excellent." This, in fact, was the key to Ferdinand's popularity. He was often called *il re Lazzarone* after the lowest class of his subjects, whose tastes he shared. Like them, he loved to eat macaroni with his hands—though he did it in the royal box at the San Carlo Theater. Like them also, he enjoyed noise and shouting and vulgarity. As for Maria Carolina, "My sister [is] dazzled by the grandeur of the court, the honors paid her, the beauty of the country, and the freedom she enjoys," the Emperor wrote.

As always, the Emperor read his sister a long lecture on her political responsibilities, and the Queen promised to take a greater interest in government. In 1775 she gave birth to an heir and entered the council of state; from that moment, life became hell for poor Ferdinand. Like her sister, the Queen of France, Maria Carolina's key principle was that the good of Austria came first, that of Naples second. If her husband resisted her suggestions, she made dreadful scenes.

Naturally, her first goal was to end all Spanish influence by removing Charles III's mouthpiece, the marchese Tanucci. When she proposed this to Ferdinand, he looked at her with horror. His father would never allow it, he said. The Queen ranted and raved, and Ferdinand wrote his father telling him that he wanted to replace Tanucci. Since the King of Spain liked having his way quite as much as Maria Carolina, he refused clearly and emphatically. Then the Queen became a Freemason. Charles III ordered her to resign, and she refused. What happened next is described by Ferdinand in a letter to his father. "She [the Queen] found me weeping and asked me what the matter was. I showed her the letter and she replied: 'So this is why you're upset? What difference can it make? He is a stubborn old blockhead who will not listen to reason and has this bee in his bonnet. Cheer up and do as I tell you.'"

The contest between the old father in Madrid

and the young wife in Naples was obviously uneven. In October, 1776, Tanucci was fired and the Queen in effect became prime minister; but it hadn't been easy. There had been dreadful public scenes during which the Queen yelled, used four-letter words, and insulted the King. In fact, the once prim and proper princess was fast becoming a shrew. "She is beginning to take on the noisy Neapolitan manner," the French minister wrote. "Added to which, she speaks all the time because she is so lively; but she speaks thoughtlessly of each person to the others, when he is out of sight, and so is not liked." Then too, her once obvious virtue had melted away in the warm Neapolitan air. While unpopular queens are always credited with lovers, whether they have them or not, it does seem certain that Maria Carolina, like Ferdinand, was soon having quick, meaningless affairs. Maria Theresa had thought that her daughter would raise Ferdinand to her level; instead, she had sunk to his.

Like Marie Antoinette, she could still charm people when she chose. An English visitor wrote:

> Her Majesty is a beautiful woman. She has the finest and most transparent complexion I ever saw; her hair is of that glossy, light chestnut I so much admire; it is by no means red; her eyes are large, brilliant and of a dark blue, her eyebrows exact and darker than her hair, her nose inclining to the aquiline, her mouth small, her lips very red (not of the Austrian thickness), her teeth beautifully white and even, and, when she smiles, she discovers two dimples which throw a finishing sweetness over her whole countenance; her shape is perfect; she is just plump enough not to appear lean; her neck is long, her deportment easy, her walk majestic, her attitude and action graceful.

This was in 1770. Soon another English visitor gave a different description:

> The Queen has something very disagreeable in her manner of speaking, moving her whole face when she talks and gesticulating violently. Her voice is very hoarse and her eyes goggle.

The charming young Queen had given way to the imperious ruler, and the change did not become her. Unlike Marie Antoinette, Maria Carolina preferred power to pleasure. She knew she was born to rule (like her mother, after all), and she loved giving orders. The only problem was that she didn't understand how governments run. She was always capable of defending a policy so as to make her viewpoint seem the only reasonable one. The following week, however, she could defend a completely different policy with the same zeal. Luckily Naples was small and unimportant, as well as prosperous. English money poured in from the first great tourist rush in history. Europe was at peace; the Queen couldn't do much harm.

Still, she realized that she needed help. Even the docile King remarked: "The Queen knows everything. And yet she makes more errors than I do, although I'm just a stupid ass." Maria Carolina asked her brother, the Grand Duke of Tuscany, to send her someone to reorganize the navy. In a fateful move, he dispatched General Acton. Within months William Hamilton reported: "It is the Queen of Naples that actually governs this country with the advice of her favorite, Prince Caramanico, and of my friend, General Acton, who is now greatly esteemed at this court."

Maria Carolina, in fact, was thoroughly taken with this forty-two-year-old English expatriate. He was experienced, reasonable, and self-assured, and he seemed oblivious to her charms. The challenge was too great to ignore. Soon Acton was minister of the navy in title, prime minister in fact, and the Queen's lover into the bargain.

Just as Maria Carolina always remained Austrian, so John Acton never forgot that he was English. A powerful navy had been the foundation of England's greatness: it should now play the same role in Naples. He promptly and efficiently reorganized the Neapolitan navy—which became very successful in defending cargo ships against the Barbary pirates, but could hardly make Naples into a great power without the economic resources necessary to sustain that role. The Queen, however, was thrilled with her kingdom's new strength at sea and felt that she was at last destined to play an international role worthy of her birth. Acton rose steadily. In 1779 he was appointed minister of war and soon began importing officers to train the new Neapolitan army regiments.

Away in Madrid, Charles III was enraged when he saw Naples moving over to the side of England, his oldest enemy, so he asked his son to dismiss Acton. The Queen retaliated by having the minister appointed field marshal. By 1780 it was understood that Acton ran the government. Since he was a foreigner, he could not officially become prime minister, but that made no difference. In 1782 the Sardinian minister wrote: "The Queen . . . sees all officials on business and listens to them, especially Acton, who is mixed up in almost everything, . . . discusses all her plans with her, and spends a great many hours in her company." Maria Carolina had all the pleasures of government without the worries. And she knew that she could trust Acton, for besides being her lover, he was austere, honest, and efficient.

Acton, however, had two major flaws: he didn't understand finance, that canker of the anciens régimes, and he behaved as if Naples were England, when in fact it was a small southern kingdom with few resources, little patriotism except of the most narrowly local sort, and no middle class. The aristocracy was frivolous and feckless; the lower orders worked as little and as seldom as possible. As for the soldiers, while they were quite willing to parade, they considered fighting dangerous and unnecessary. Try as he might, Acton was building on sand.

Convinced that she was a second Maria Theresa, with Acton as her Kaunitz, Maria Carolina felt vastly superior to her sister in France. When Ferdinand cut up rough, as he sometimes did, she knew just how to manage him. First she

An Eruption of Vesuvius, a plate from the *Encyclopédie.*
Thomas J. Watson Library,
The Metropolitan Museum of Art, New York

tried sex. The King went mad at the sight of a woman's arm in a long, tight glove, so when he proved difficult, Maria Carolina reached for the nearest glove. This strategy had its drawbacks: she produced twelve children by 1792, and all those pregnancies made her look older than her age. People no longer found her beautiful; what they saw now was an almost grotesquely long face with goggling eyes, an interminable nose, and a ravaged look.

The Queen's other method of dealing with the King also worked well but could not be used too often, for it consisted of faking a disagreement with Acton. The minister would propose a course of action, Maria Carolina would oppose it, and the King would decide in favor of the minister. Feeling strong, independent, and statesmanlike, the King would recover his good humor.

Saint Non. *View of Pompeii,* a plate from *Voyage pittoresque.* General Research Division, The New York Public Library, Astor, Lenox and Tilden Foundations

It was all rather like opera buffa: the splendid, dissolute court, the good-natured, lazy people, the sunny Bay of Naples, the throngs of tourists. Acton might toil away, but no one else took Naples seriously—except, perhaps, its most celebrated foreign resident. Sir William Hamilton had been the English minister to the court of Naples since 1764, and he had become a fixture. Everyone liked him, from the monarchs and Ac-

ton on down. He knew Naples better than anyone and was happy to enlighten the noble English travelers who came in numbers to see the landscape, the Roman ruins at Pompeii and Herculaneum, and with luck, an eruption of Mount Vesuvius. In 1786 Sir William added a new attraction to his famous collection of Roman artifacts: the splendidly alive Emma Hart. It was impossible to visit Naples without seeing the minister and

his pretty protégée. Like every other visitor, Goethe was immensely taken with both. He wrote:

> Hamilton is a person of universal taste and has found rest at last in a most beautiful companion, a masterpiece of that great artist, Nature. . . . She is an Englishwoman about twenty years old. . . . The old Knight has had a Greek costume made for her, which becomes her extremely. Dressed in this, and letting her hair loose, and taking a couple of shawls, she exhibits every possible variety of posture, expression, and look so that, at last, the spectator almost fancies it is a dream. One beholds there in perfection, in movement, in ravishing variety all that the greatest of artists have rejoiced in being able to produce. Standing, sitting, kneeling, lying down, grave or sad, playful, exulting, repentant, wanton, menacing, anxious—all mental states follow rapidly one after the other. With wonderful taste, she suits the folding of her veil to each expression and with the same handkerchief makes every kind of headdress. The old Knight . . . thinks he can discern in her a resemblance to all the most famous antiques, all the beautiful profiles on the Sicilian coins.

It was impossible to visit Naples without seeing the beautiful Emma. And with luck, the visitor managed to watch her without speaking to her, for she was deeply, dreadfully stupid.

It seemed as if this little world would go on forever. Not even the beginning of the French Revolution seriously disturbed the Queen; she simply felt superior for having managed affairs better than her sister. And so, when Joseph II died in February, 1790, it seemed like a good time for a working holiday, and the King and Queen of Naples went to Germany for the coronation of Leopold II, Joseph's successor and brother. In addition, the Queen's daughter Maria Theresa was to be married to Leopold's son, the archduke Francis. The trip lasted for eight months, all of which were blissful for Maria Carolina. Not only was she greeted everywhere with the greatest respect, but she felt that she had accomplished the task set by her mother. Naples was pro-Austrian and more respected than it had ever been. Now the alliance was being strengthened by the marriage of her daughter to the Austrian Crown Prince.

The only flaw in Maria Carolina's happiness was a disagreement with Acton. The recently appointed foreign minister had been pushing for an alliance with England. Maria Carolina was against it because she thought it would weaken the ties to Austria. As soon as she returned to Naples, she appointed a new chief of police to counterbalance the ex-favorite.

This, as it turned out, was an unwise move. Luigi de' Medici, while encouraging the Queen to overspend, played a double game by secretly protecting a group of liberals who wanted a revolution on the French model. The result was that the court lived in a state of harrowing suspense for the next few years. By now the developments in France terrified and angered the Queen; the execution of Louis XVI had been bad enough, but that of Marie Antoinette transformed her hatred of France into a burning obsession. In addition, she feared that a revolutionary movement might develop in Naples.

"This infamous Revolution has made me cruel," Maria Carolina wrote in 1794, and it was true. Under her rule the character of the monarchy began to change. What had been a paternal, disorganized, well-meaning autocracy became a dictatorship, with police spies, arbitrary arrests, and loyalty tests. And at the helm, visible to all, the Queen represented everything that people hated about the ancien régime. On a personal level also, Maria Carolina found herself caught at her own game. In the past the scenes she had made were deliberate, but now her temper became hysterical and uncontrolled, her moods changing violently and rapidly. Nothing was left of the amiable, virtuous archduchess.

Still, there was one positive development in the Queen's life. Sir William Hamilton, having married the beautiful Emma, was able to bring her to court. Like Marie Antoinette, the Queen had a susceptibility to beautiful young women. Soon she was having the most blissful love affair with her ever-willing "cara miladi," writing her constantly and consulting her on the political situation. "Send me some news, political and private," Emma was soon asking Greville, "for, against my will, and owing to my situation here,

Romney. *Lady Hamilton.*
Copyright The Frick Collection,
New York

I am got into politicks and I wish to have news for our dear much loved Queen, whom I adore. Nor can I live without her, for she is to me another friend [Sir William being the first 'friend'] and everything. If you could know her as I do, how you would adore her! For she is the first woman in the world; and her heart is most excellent." Since Naples had signed an alliance with England at this time, nothing could have been more convenient than for the Queen to have an affair with the wife of the British minister. And when Nelson sailed into the Bay and was in turn smitten by Emma's charms, the Queen was able to feel that she had a strong defender.

In the meantime Bonaparte was conquering Italy, and the Queen, who loathed everything he represented, could not help admiring him. Still, she exploded when Nelson's victory at Trafalgar seemed sure to leave him stranded in Egypt forever. "It is not possible," Lady Hamilton wrote, "to describe her transports; she wept, she kissed her husband, her children, walked frantically about the room, burst into tears again, and again kissed and embraced every person near her, exclaiming 'Oh, brave Nelson! Oh, God! Bless and protect our brave deliverer.'"

In the long run, however, the victory turned out to be a disaster. In November, 1798, emboldened by Nelson's success and by his advice, Ferdinand decided to liberate Rome from the French yoke. The Neapolitan army set forth and actually reached the city, only to fall back in panic as soon as it met mild opposition. The debacle was complete: within days the French army had entered Naples. As for the royal family, it had set sail for Sicily on Nelson's ships.

Her arrival in Sicily marked the end of Maria Carolina's power. Ferdinand may have been slow, but eventually it occurred to him that the net result of his wife's rule was the loss of half his kingdom. He moved out of the royal palace to a country villa and made it plain that the Queen's day was over. Even the reconquest of Naples in June, 1799, hardly changed the situation. Now the King sometimes listened to his wife, but not often enough to support any steady policy. In 1800 the Hamiltons were recalled to England;

Maria Carolina had lost her main support.

Court life continued, so that the Queen still had a ceremonial role. The French came back in January, 1806, however, and this time they stayed. In Palermo Maria Carolina found herself completely isolated. The new British minister, Lord William Bentinck, loathed her and saw to it that she was neglected. Finally, in 1813, he became so hostile that the Queen had to go. She set off for Vienna, but since war was raging across half of Europe, she had to go through Turkey and Russia. It took her eight months to reach Austria, and when she finally arrived in Vienna early in February, 1814, she turned out to be something of an embarrassment. This last living daughter of the great Maria Theresa was extremely popular. Since the allies were reluctant to take Naples back from Murat, who was now fighting against Napoleon, it was thought better that she reside at Hetzendorff, a pleasant castle near Schönbrunn. In May the ex-empress Marie Louise arrived back in Vienna and met her grandmother for the first time (she was the daughter of Maria Carolina's daughter Maria Theresa and the emperor Francis). By then the old Queen's hatred of England was so fierce that she was beginning to feel sympathy for Napoleon—a reversal in feeling undoubtedly eased by the Emperor's defeat and abdication.

Maria Carolina had lost none of her outspokenness or her courage. Méneval, Napoleon's ex-secretary, was now part of Marie Louise's suite. He wrote after meeting the old lady:

> The Queen, who had been the declared enemy of Napoleon in the time of his prosperity, and whose opinion could not be suspected of partiality, professed a high regard for his great qualities. . . . She said that, formerly, she had cause to complain of him, that he had persecuted her and wounded her pride . . . but that now he was in adversity, she forgot everything. She could not repress her indignation at the maneuvers to break up a marriage in which her granddaughter should glory. . . . She added that if their reunion was opposed, Marie Louise should tie her bedsheets to her window and escape in disguise.

It was a noble stand for the old Queen to take, but it was out of joint with the times; perhaps it was just as well that she died suddenly on September 7, 1814.

No one missed Maria Carolina. Ferdinand eventually married his mistress. Metternich, for whom Maria Carolina had been an added burden, was profoundly relieved. The legend of her wickedness began to grow. Soon she was represented as a cross between Messalina and Catherine de' Medici, as a depraved tyrant whose hands were red with blood and whose debauchery was beyond description. It was, in fact, a typical case of the nineteenth century judging the eighteenth. By Victorian standards, Maria Carolina was indeed a monster, but she hadn't lived in that hypocritical and repressed era. While she undoubtedly overestimated her powers, she led a life singularly free of pretense. And by the criteria of her time, she did not do so badly. In the end, it was not her ultimate failure that so affronted her critics, but rather the fact that she claimed all the rights, all the liberties, all the understanding which came as the birthright of the eighteenth-century woman.

"Women reigned then," Mme Vigée-Lebrun had written of the ancien régime; and she went on to say, "but the Revolution has toppled their throne." In France and, as the consequences multiplied, in most of Europe, the Revolution ended the high culture in which women had become so powerful. Women went to the guillotine as bravely as men, but an aroused populace had little taste for refined manners or intellectual pursuits. When the character of the nineteenth century had fully emerged, money had replaced culture, and women had again become mere chattels.

By the end of the nineteenth century it was well understood that women were fragile creatures with frivolous minds who could not cope with the rough-and-tumble of everyday life. The laws, in France, at least, were as discriminatory toward women as they had been in the eighteenth century—but now they were implemented rather than ignored.

Worse, a new double standard prevailed in the nineteenth century. It was all right for men to have affairs, but adulterous women were considered beyond the pale if their misdeeds were discovered. It was proper for men to manage the world, but women were thought unfeminine if they even offered an opinion. Finally, a husband who depleted his wife's dowry—often spending it on a demimondaine—was admired for his virility, while a wife who looked after the family's fortune and increased it was condemned for her rapacity. It is no wonder, therefore, that eighteenth-century customs aroused universal scorn: liberty always seems detestable to a shackled society.

Only in our own time have women reclaimed those rights which custom, if not law, granted during the Enlightenment. Once again the double standard is despised: women claim—and largely receive—the same sexual freedom as men. Today, however, divorce has become an easy option, and in consequence the married state is a choice rather than an obligation. Once again women—such as Golda Meir, Margaret Thatcher, Indira Gandhi—have taken their place as political leaders. Better yet, it is unquestionably easier for a woman today to earn a living or pursue an artistic career than it was during the Enlightenment. The eighteenth-century woman, however, had one great advantage: she expected equality in fact, yet remained entitled to the respect and the consideration so obviously due to the superior sex.

Mme de Pompadour. *Dawn,* engraving after Boucher. The marquise was a skillful engraver and often worked from designs specially made for her by Boucher. The Metropolitan Museum of Art, New York. Harris Brisbane Dick Fund, 1917 (17.3.1074)

Source Notes

For the author's full name, place and date of publication, and other relevant bibliographic data for the following notes, please refer to the Bibliography. The initial number in the following entries indicates the text page on which the quotation appears.

Chapter 1

11. *It is indeed:* Mme des Ursins, in Maintenon, *Lettres inédites de Madame de Maintenon et de Madame la princesse Des Ursins.*

12. *[Mme des Ursins] is witty:* Quoted in Cermakian, *La princesse Des Ursins.*

13. *I have the honor:* Des Ursins, *Lettres inédites.*

14. *I hardly know:* Quoted in Cermakian, *La princesse.*

14. *She had vast:* Saint-Simon, *Mémoires.*

14. *the princess dealt:* Cermakian, *La princesse.*

15. *Where now are:* Quoted in ibid.

15. *I may tell:* Ibid.

18. *The meeting was:* Ibid.

18. *Our two Kings:* Maintenon, *Lettres à d'Aubigné et à Madame Des Ursins.*

18. *It is no life:* Ibid.

18. *I have received:* Maintenon, *Lettres inédites.*

18. *We hear such:* Ibid.

18. *You will be:* Ibid.

20. *talked to him like a father:* Saint-Simon, *Mémoires.*

20. *Her wit:* Ibid.

22. *Madame la duchesse:* Ibid.

22. *Suddenly she saw:* Ibid.

23. *She was a prodigy:* Ibid.

25. *Babet has passed away:* Cited in Roujon, *La fille du régent.*

Chapter 2

27. *the graces of:* Walpole, *Correspondence with Madame Du Deffand.*

27. *What else shall:* Ibid.

28. *This passion made:* Quoted in Ferval, *Madame Du Deffand.*

28. *No one could:* Ibid.

28. *Nobody has more:* Staal-Delaunay, *Mémoires.*

31. *Whenever you confide:* Mme du Deffand, quoted in Walpole, *Correspondence.*

32. *Mme la marquise:* Ibid.

32. *Mme de . . . is:* Ibid.

32. *Often she falls:* Ibid.

33. *You could not:* Ibid.

34. *What cowardice:* Ibid.

34. *I am just like:* Ibid.

34. *M. le duc de Chevreuse:* Ibid.

34. *I esteem no one:* Letter from Mme du Deffand, quoted in Ferval, *Du Deffand.*

34. *The only misfortune:* Ibid.

36. *All the masquerade balls:* Luynes, *Mémoires.*

37. *She was tall, svelte:* See particularly the description by Georges Leroy, quoted in Nolhac, "Les portraits de la Pompadour," in *L'Art et les Artistes,* vol. 2 (Paris, 1906).

41. *As soon as the King:* Luynes, *Mémoires.*

43. *a new edition of Corneille's Rodogune:* The unusual location of the printing press is revealed by M. de Marigny's notes on the title page of his copy of the book and transcribed in Leturcq, *Notice sur Jacques Guay.*

44. *Luckily we have accounts:* The expenses are itemized in Cordey, *Inventaire des biens de Madame de Pompadour.*

46. *The life I lead:* Quoted in Michel, *Prestigieuse marquise de Pompadour.*

46. *alone near the fireplace:* Ibid.

47. *Everything which has been:* Ibid.

Chapter 3

51. *The unprejudiced observer:* Wolff, *Historie van Mejuffrouw Sara Burgerhart.*

51. *She has much nonfeminine:* Ibid.

56. *He has nice hair:* Quoted in Herold, *Mistress to an Age.*

56. *the wit, the beauty:* Gibbon, *The Works of Edward Gibbon.*

57. *sighed as a lover* and *the remedies:* Ibid.

57. *I cannot begin:* Quoted in Herold, *Mistress.*

57. *I blush at:* Ibid.

58. *I came to Paris:* Quoted in Corbaz, *Madame Necker.* Mme Necker's letters quoted throughout Corbaz are deposited in the archives of Coppet.

58–59. *They will bore each other:* Ibid.

60. *O my Jacques:* Ibid.

60. *Picture to yourself:* Ibid.

61. *[Mme Necker's] fame grows:* Mme de Vermenoux, quoted in Corbaz, *Necker.*

62. *A Friday does not:* Galiani, *Correspondance inédite.*

62. *She never tired:* Staël-Holstein, *Corinne.*

63. *Oh, my God:* Quoted in Corbaz, *Necker.*

63. *It was not for us:* Ibid.

66. *the budget was made visible:* See Necker, *Compte-rendu au roi.*

66. *Our Hôtel-Dieu:* Quoted in Corbaz, *Necker.*

66. *[We have] airy rooms:* Ibid.

Chapter 4

69. *This woman is well known:* Quoted in Goncourt, *Mademoiselle Clairon,* from the police report in the Archives Nationales, Paris.

71. *One is alarmed:* Ibid.

71. *a brochure appeared entitled:* See [Gaillard de la Bataille?], *Histoire de Mademoiselle Cronel dite Frétillon.*

73. *The tone of your:* Quoted in Goncourt, *Clairon.*

74. *All the agréables:* *L'Observateur des Spectacles* (Paris, 1744).

74. *He's become completely:* Quoted in Goncourt, *Clairon.*

76. *A courageous actress:* Ibid.

77. *This tragedy is not:* Ibid.

77. *Mlle Clairon was incomparable:* Ibid.

77. *If you could only see:* Ibid.

79. *Although I am ready:* Quoted in Haussonville, *Femmes d'autrefois.* The letter is deposited in the archives of Coppet.

81. *She was nonchalantly:* Quoted in Levron, *Le destin de Madame Du Barry.*

82. *Although Madame de Pompadour:* Talleyrand-Périgord, *Mémoires.*

82. *I have never in my:* Quoted in Levron, *Le destin.*

86. *I'm told that:* Ibid.

86. *Vous connaissez, je crois:* Cited in Cantrel, *Nouvelles à la main sur la comtesse Du Barry.*

86. *worth over 450,000 livres:* It fetched that price when Mme du Barry sold it after the King's death in 1774.

86. *to draw ... for all her household expenses:* See Welschinger, ed., *Les bijoux de Madame Du Barry.*

88. *she owned over 140 large diamonds:* Ibid.

89. *It is ... scandalous:* Quoted in Levron, *Le destin.*

89. *You take good care:* Ibid.

92. *... received me in the most:* Vigée-Lebrun, *Souvenirs.*

92. *If Louis XV had lived:* Ibid.

93. *You have before you:* Quoted in Levron, *Le destin.*

Chapter 5

98. *Let us therefore:* Letter of John Adams, quoted in Bobbé, *Abigail Adams.*

98. *The great distance:* Adams, ed., *Familiar Letters of John Adams and His Wife Abigail Adams During the Revolution,* letter of August 19, 1774.

98. *Not a Tory but hides:* Ibid., letter of September 14, 1774.

99. *I dare not express:* Ibid., letter of October 16, 1774.

99. *'Tis a little more than:* Ibid., letter of March 8, 1778.

99. *I would not have:* Ibid., letter of July 6, 1775.

99. *The distresses of the:* Ibid., letter of May 7, 1775.

100. *I long to hear* and *And by the way:* Ibid., letter of March 31, 1776.

100. *I cannot say that:* Ibid., letter of May 7, 1776.

100. *I have been in:* Ibid., letter of March 2, 1776.

100. *I went to bed:* Ibid., letter of March 5, 1776.

101. *Last Thursday:* Ibid., letter of July 21, 1776.

101. *un jeune homme:* Quoted in Bobbé, *Adams.*

101. *It would be futile:* Adams, ed., *Familiar Letters,* letter of April 12, 1778.

102. *inconvenient and required too many servants:* See Adams, *The Adams Family in Auteuil.*

102. *The dresses and beauty:* Adams, *Letters of Mrs. Adams,* letter to her sister, Mrs. Cranch.

102. *I could scarcely believe:* Quoted in Whitney, *Abigail Adams.*

104. *Mama ... are Tories born:* Cited in Stokes, *The Devonshire House Circle.*

106. *The Drawing Room was:* Coke, *The Letters and Journals of Lady Mary Coke.*

106. *The Duchess of Devonshire effaces:* Walpole, *The Works of Horatio Walpole.*

106. *kindness embellished by* and *possessed an ardent:* Quoted in Stokes, *Devonshire House.*

106. *I wish there were:* Walpole, *Works.*

107. *Would you believe:* Anecdote related in Cecil, *The Young Melbourne.*

107. *He din'd here:* Letter, quoted in Stokes, *Devonshire House.*

107. *No Rose could ever:* Cited in ibid.

107. *I have always thought:* Letter, quoted in ibid.

110. *Charles is unquestionably:* Ibid.

113. *Only think, Sir, it was:* Cited in ibid.

114. *Lord, Sir, it was:* Ibid.

114. *She canvass'd all:* Ibid.

114. *Your eyes are so:* Letter, quoted in ibid.

114. *And hail the chapel:* Cited in Foster, ed., *The Two Duchesses.*

114. *I am wretched:* Ibid.

114. *I do not find:* Burney, *The Diary and Letters of Madame d'Arblay.*

115. *I now saw the Duchess:* Ibid.

Chapter 6

118. *It is up to you:* Arneth and Geffroy, eds., *Correspondance secrète entre Marie-Thérèse et le comte de Mercy-Argenteau.*

119. *a court presentation dress:* Description from an invoice sent by Mlle Bertin, quoted in Nouvion, *Un ministre des modes sous Louis XVI.*

119. *a hat with a fine-pleated lace:* Ibid.

119-20. *On May 28* and *there was a little Bohemian:* Oberkirch, *Mémoires.*

120. *A noble lady came:* Arneth and Geffroy, eds., *Correspondance secrète* (1865).

122. *It is fair to say:* Campan, *Mémoires sur la vie de Marie-Antoinette.*

122. *This was not the portrait:* Arneth and Geffroy, eds., *Correspondance secrète entre Marie-Thérèse.*

126. *What, Monsieur:* Quoted in Nouvion, *Un ministre.*

130. *beauty could really make:* Vigée-Lebrun, *Souvenirs.*

130. *Mlle Vigée is by way:* Le Brun, *Almanach historique et raisonné des architectes, peintres, sculpteurs, graveurs, et cizeleurs.*

131. *It wasn't that M. Lebrun:* Vigée-Lebrun, *Souvenirs.*

131. *Mme Lebrun is pretty:* *Mémoires Secrets,* vol. 22.

131. *The party, as she quickly explained:* Vigée-Lebrun, *Souvenirs.*

133. *As I had a horror:* Ibid.

134. *I tried as hard:* Ibid.

134. *Le Brun, de la beauté:* Cited in Hautecoeur, *Madame Vigée-Lebrun.*

135. *I know nothing about:* Quoted in Vigée-Lebrun, *Souvenirs.*

135. *Your big portrait:* Arneth and Geffroy, eds., *Correspondance secrète entre Marie-Thérèse.*

137. *My heart was beating:* Vigée-Lebrun, *Souvenirs.*

138. *The Academy, deferring:* Quoted in Joseph Baillio, "Marie-Antoinette et ses enfants par Madame Vigée-Le Brun," in *L'Oeil* (March and May, 1981).

138. *Many people:* Quoted in Nolhac, *Madame Vigée-Le Brun.*

140. *No one can:* Vigée-Lebrun, *Souvenirs.*

140. *I would seem vain:* Quoted in Hautecoeur, *Vigée-Lebrun.*

Chapter 7

143. *We only lived:* Wilhelmina, *The Misfortunate Margravine.*

144. *She is still with me:* Ibid.

144. *Never has there:* Quoted in Fauchier-Magnan, *Les petites cours d'Allemagne au XVIIIème siècle.*

144. *I am as close:* Ibid.

144. *known for his debauchery:* Wilhelmina, *Misfortunate Margravine.*

145. *I have had that scoundrel:* Ibid.

145. *We all ran:* Ibid.

145. *... tall and well built:* Ibid.

146. *Imagine monsters:* Savine, ed., *Une résidence allemande au XVIIIème siècle.*

146. *I found myself:* Ibid.

147. *The great tenderness:* Ibid.

147. *You and I, my dear:* Ibid.

147. *a pretty little library:* Quoted in Fauchier-Magnan, *Petites cours.*

148. *I thank you a thousand:* Ibid.

148. *Your Royal Highness:* Voltaire, *Correspondance.*

148. *I have seen a court:* Quoted in Fauchier-Magnan, *Petites cours.*

148. *You have every kind:* Ibid.

149. *We have a great need:* Ibid.

149. *Europe suffers:* Ibid.

149. *You can easily judge:* Ibid.

150. *She is a most amiable:* Mann, *Life and Works of Horace Mann.*

152. *His Sicilian Majesty:* Quoted in Acton, *The Bourbons of Naples*.

153. *Dorme comm'un amazzata:* Ibid.

153. *Er ist ein recht:* Manuscript correspondence of Joseph II in the Haus-, Hof-, und Staatsarchiv, Vienna.

153. *Although an ugly prince:* Ibid.

153. *My sister [is] dazzled:* Ibid.

153. *She [the Queen] found me:* Quoted in Acton, *Bourbons*.

154. *She is beginning:* Ibid.

154. *Her Majesty is:* Miller, *Letters from Italy*.

154. *The Queen has:* Swinburne, *Travels in the Two Sicilies*.

154. *The Queen knows:* Quoted in Acton, *Bourbons*.

154. *It is the Queen of Naples:* Ibid.

155. *The Queen . . . sees:* Ibid.

158. *Hamilton is a person:* Goethe, *Italian Journey*.

160. *Send me some news:* Quoted in Acton, *Bourbons*.

160. *It is not possible:* Ibid.

160. *The Queen, who had:* Méneval, *Marie-Louise et la cour d'Autriche entre les deux abdications*.

161. *Women reigned then:* Vigée-Lebrun, *Souvenirs*.

Boucher. *Decorative motif.* The fluid, twisting forms are typical of the
Rococo style. The Metropolitan Museum of Art, New York.
Harris Brisbane Dick Fund, 1951 (51.600.1086)

Selected Bibliography

Acton, Harold. *The Bourbons of Naples.* London, 1956.

Adams, Abigail. *The Adams Family in Auteuil, 1784–1785: As Told in the Letters of Abigail Adams.* Introduction and notes by Howard C. Rice, Jr. Boston, 1956.

_____. *Letters of Mrs. Adams, the Wife of John Adams.* Edited by Charles Francis Adams. 4th ed. Boston, 1848.

Adams, Charles Francis, ed. *Familiar Letters of John Adams and His Wife Abigail Adams During the Revolution.* New York, 1876.

Arneth, Alfred von, and Geffroy, Auguste, eds. *Correspondance secrète.* Paris, 1865.

_____. *Correspondance secrète entre Marie-Thérèse et le comte de Mercy-Argenteau.* Paris, 1874–75.

Bobbé, Dorothie. *Abigail Adams: The Second First Lady.* New York, 1929.

Burney, Fanny (Frances d'Arblay). *The Diary and Letters of Madame d'Arblay.* Boston, 1842–46.

Campan, Jeanne Louise Henriette. *Mémoires sur la vie de Marie-Antoinette.* Paris, 1822.

Cantrel, Emile. *Nouvelles à la main sur la comtesse Du Barry.* Paris, 1861.

Carré, Henri. *Mademoiselle, fille du régent, duchesse de Berry.* Paris, 1936.

Caylus, Marie Marguerite Valois de Vilette de Murçay, Comtesse de. *Souvenirs.* Amsterdam, 1770. Edited by Bernard Noël. Paris, 1965.

Cecil, David. *The Young Melbourne, and the Story of His Marriage with Caroline Lamb.* London, 1939.

Cermakian, Marianne. *La princesse Des Ursins: sa vie et ses lettres.* Paris, 1969.

Clairon. *Mémoires de Mademoiselle Clairon.* Paris, 1822.

Coke, Mary. *The Letters and Journals of Lady Mary Coke.* Edited by J. A. Home. Edinburgh, 1889–96.

Corbaz, André. *Madame Necker.* Lausanne, 1945.

Cordey, Jean. *Inventaire des biens de Madame de Pompadour.* Paris, 1939.

Cuthell, Edith E. *Wilhelmina, Margravine of Baireuth.* London, 1905.

Des Ursins, Anne Marie de La Trémoille, Princesse. *Lettres inédites.* Edited by Auguste Geffroy. Paris, 1859.

Fauchier-Magnan, Adrien. *Les petites cours d'Allemagne au XVIIIème siècle.* Paris, 1947.

Ferval, Claude. *Madame Du Deffand.* Paris, 1933.

Foster, Vere, ed. *The Two Duchesses: Georgiana, Duchess of Devonshire, Elizabeth, Duchess of Devonshire.* London, 1898.

[Gaillard de la Bataille, Pierre Alexandre?]. *Histoire de Mademoiselle Cronel dite Frétillon.* The Hague, 1741.

Galiani, Ferdinando. *Correspondance inédite de l'abbé Ferdinand Galiani.* Paris, 1818.

Gibbon, Edward. *The Works of Edward Gibbon.* Edited by J. B. Bury, John Murray, and others. New York, 1906–07.

Goethe, Johann Wolfgang von. *Italian Journey.* Translated by W. H. Auden and Elizabeth Mayer. New York, 1962.

Goncourt, Edmond de. *Mademoiselle Clairon, d'après ses correspondances et les rapports de police du temps.* Paris, 1890.

Goncourt, Edmond et Jules de. *La femme au XVIIIème siècle.* Paris, 1862.

Haussonville, Gabriel Paul Othenin de Cléron, Comte d'. *Femmes d'autrefois; hommes d'aujourd'hui.* Paris, 1912.

Hautecoeur, Louis. *Madame Vigée-Lebrun.* Paris, 1926.

Herold, J. Christopher. *Love in Five Temperaments.* London, 1961.

_____. *Mistress to an Age: A Life of Madame de Staël.* Indianapolis, 1958.

La Trémoille, Louis Charles, Duc de. *Madame Des Ursins et la succession d'Espagne.* Paris, 1902–07.

La Varende, Jean de. *Le mariage de Mademoiselle et ses suites.* Paris, 1956.

Le Brun, Jean Baptiste Pierre. *Almanach historique et raisonné des architectes, peintres, sculpteurs, graveurs, et cizeleurs.* Paris, 1776–77.

Leturcq, Jean François. *Notice sur Jacques Guay, graveur sur pierres fines du roi Louis XV.* Paris, 1873.

Levron, Jacques. *Le destin de Madame Du Barry.* Paris, 1961.

Luynes, Charles Philippe d'Albert, Duc de. *Mémoires.* Paris, 1860–65.

Maintenon, Françoise d'Aubigné, Marquise de. *Lettres à d'Aubigné et à Madame Des Ursins.* Introduction and notes by Gonzague Truc. Paris, 1921.

_____. *Lettres inédites de Madame de Maintenon et de Madame la princesse Des Ursins.* Paris, 1826.

Mann, Horace. *Life and Works of Horace Mann.* Edited by Mary Mann. Boston, 1865–68.

Méneval, Napoléon Joseph, Baron de. *Marie-Louise et la cour d'Autriche entre les deux abdications.* Paris, 1909.

Michel, Ludovic. *Prestigieuse marquise de Pompadour.* Paris, 1972.

Miller, Anne. *Letters from Italy.* 2nd ed. London, 1777.

Necker, Jacques. *Compte-rendu au roi.* Paris, 1781.

Nolhac, Pierre de. *Madame Vigée-Le Brun.* Paris, 1908.

Nouvion, Pierre de. *Un ministre des modes sous Louis XVI, Mademoiselle Bertin.* Paris, 1911.

Oberkirch, Henriette Louise, Baronne d'. *Mémoires.* Paris, 1853. Edited by Suzanne Burkard. Paris, 1970.

Roujon, Jacques. *La fille du régent.* Paris, 1935.

Saint-Simon, Louis de Rouvroy, Duc de. *Mémoires.* London and Paris, 1788. Edited by Gonzague Truc. Bibliothèque de la Pléiade. Paris, 1947–61.

Savine, Albert, ed. *Une résidence allemande au XVIIIème siècle, souvenirs de la margrave de Bayreuth.* Paris, 1910.

Staal-Delaunay, Marguerite Jeanne, Baronne de. *Mémoires.* London, 1755. Edited by Gérard Doscot. Paris, 1970.

Staël-Holstein, Germaine Necker, Baronne de (Madame de Staël). *Corinne.* Paris, 1807.

Stokes, Hugh. *The Devonshire House Circle.* London, 1917.

Strachey, Lytton. *Books and Characters.* London, 1922.

Swinburne, Henry. *Travels in the Two Sicilies.* 2nd ed. London, 1790.

Talleyrand-Périgord, Charles Maurice de. *Mémoires du prince de Talleyrand.* Edited by the Duc de Broglie. Paris, 1891–92.

Vigée-Lebrun, Louise Elisabeth. *Souvenirs.* Paris, 1835–37.

Voltaire, Arouet de. *Correspondance.* Kehl, 1785. Edited by Theodore Besterman. Geneva, 1953–65.

Walpole, Horace. *Correspondence with Madame Du Deffand.* Edited by W. S. Lewis and Warren Hunting Smith. New Haven, 1939.

_____. *The Works of Horatio Walpole.* Edited by Mary Berry. London, 1798.

Welschinger, Henri, ed. *Les bijoux de Madame Du Barry: documents inédits.* Paris, 1881.

Whitney, Janet. *Abigail Adams.* Boston, 1947.

Wilhelmina, Margravine of Bayreuth. *The Misfortunate Margravine: The Early Memoirs of Wilhelmina.* London, 1970.

Wolff, Elizabeth. *Historie van Mejuffrouw Sara Burgerhart.* The Hague, 1782.

Photographs of objects in The Metropolitan Museum of Art by Sheldan Collins, Lynton Gardiner, Alexander Mikhailovich, Walter J. F. Yee, The Photograph Studio, The Metropolitan Museum of Art

Composition by LCR Graphics, Inc., New York
Printing by Rae Publishing Co., Inc., Cedar Grove, New Jersey
Binding by American Book-Stratford Press, Inc., Saddle Brook, New Jersey